HOME OWNERSHIP: THE DIVERSITY OF EXPERIENCE

Home Ownership: The Diversity of Experience

JOHN DOLING
Department of Administration
University of Birmingham

BRUCE STAFFORD
Environmental Health and Housing
University of Salford

Gower
Aldershot · Brookfield USA · Hong Kong · Singapore · Sydney

Published by

Gower Publishing Company Limited,
Gower House, Croft Road, Aldershot,
Hants. GU11 3HR England.

Gower Publishing Company
Old Post Road, Brookfield, Vermont 05036, USA.

ISBN 0-566-05650-X

Phototypeset in Times, using the Compugraphic MCS8400 Phototypesetter at the Centre for Computing and Computer Science, University of Birmingham.

Contents

Preface

The election of the first Thatcher government in 1979 together with other developments at the national and international levels heralded a period of rapid social and economic change in Britain. These changes have touched all aspects of modern life and have been particularly marked in the employment sphere, where both the level and the rate of unemployment have increased significantly during the last decade. The housing market has not been immune to these wider changes because it does not, and cannot, operate in splendid isolation.

In this book we focus on recent changes in home ownership and the labour market. Home ownership is now the dominant tenure in Britain and well documented increases in mortgage default and property disrepair, for example, suggest some sort of link with the labour market not least because money, in the form of wages or salaries, is for many people required to avert both problems. Our concern is, firstly, to describe home ownership in the 1980s - and the picture which emerges is different from that of its traditional 'safe as houses' image - and secondly, to understand and explain the changes which we observe. This book should add to our knowledge of the housing system in Britain, and be of help to policymakers. Although it must be stressed that we offer no policy nostrums or panacea.

The empirical evidence presented in this book is at two levels: national and local. The local material is taken from a research project of recent buyers in the City of Coventry. This study was sponsored by Joseph Rowntree Memorial Trust, and was an extension of previous research carried out by the authors with others, notably Valerie Karn.

The relevance of Coventry as a case study lies with its changing fortunes. In the first two decades following the Second World War it was, as in much of the inter war period, a symbol of prosperity. Its economic base was concentrated on growth industries, particularly vehicles. There was generally a shortage of labour so the unemployment rate was lower than elsewhere in the country and wage rates were higher. Population grew rapidly as semi skilled and skilled workers flocked into the city, and it continued to expand. Notwithstanding the strong bias towards manual employment - a group less well represented nationally in home ownership than those in white collar jobs - by the end of the 1960s already two thirds of Coventry's households were home owners. So Coventry was fairly unusual, in national terms, in having a largely blue collar labour force employed at high wages and using that purchasing power to become home owners. As the economy has changed nationally, so has it in Coventry where since the mid 1960s there have been progressively more fundamental shocks. By the 1980s unemployment was higher than nationally, and wage rates lower. People no longer flock into Coventry, but many of Coventry's residents look elsewhere to meet their employment needs. The proportion of home owners in the city has not changed greatly, but the former prosperity which supported the tenure has declined.

Thus the Coventry survey, like this book, is not simply an account of low income home ownership. Our concern is also with the consequences of economic change for home ownership. Published data are used to demonstrate national trends, and the Coventry survey results are used as a case study to highlight and develop our argument. The Coventry data help us to understand some of the processes at work which are lost in aggregated national data.

Acknowledgements

In part this book draws upon research the authors conducted on home ownership in Coventry. During the course of that study we benefitted from discussions with, and obtained information from, a number of people. We would like to record our gratitude for their help. From Coventry City Council they include: Mr H. Farrand and Mr Ken Pallaser (Environmental Health); Shirley Trafford (Planning); Lorraine Knibb, Mr V. Ashby and Mr James (Homes and Property Services); and the staff of the local history library. In addition we are particularly grateful to Mr Ralph Butcher of the GIA team for his considerable assistance and support. Outside of the local authority we owe a debt of gratitude to the staff at the Coventry Workshop; Robin Cooper of Warwick Estates and President of the National Association of Estate Agents; and the 302 households who gave their time to the completion of a long questionnaire. Valuable help was given by John Cope with survey work and Joan Morgan with typing reports and general secretarial work. The data were analysed on the mainframe at the University of Birmingham using SPSS. We have also received assistance from Valerie Karn, Professor of Environmental Health and Housing at the University of Salford. Notwithstanding such assistance the responsibility for any errors of omission or commission rests, of course, with the authors.

We would also like to thank the Housing Centre Trust for permission to reproduce a diagram from Gow (1985) 'Maintenance and modernisation – a discipline in search of a philosophy?', *Housing Review*, November/December, pp. 187-188.

Finally, our thanks to the Joseph Rowntree Memorial Trust who sponsored the survey of recent buyers in Coventry.

John Doling
Bruce Stafford
October 1987

1 Introduction

The benefits of home ownership

The aim of this book is to question the basis of the ideology dominant in modern Britain that home ownership is invariably a 'good' thing. This has not generally been taken to mean that all home owners have enjoyed the same level of 'goodness'. For one thing the factual evidence of wide variation in sizes, locations and quality is all too clear. But the tacit assumption has been that, although some home owners get better housing than others, what they all enjoy is varying levels of 'goodness'. All home owners, in other words, have been seen as benefitting from their tenure position and in a way which those who rent do not necessarily do.

Perhaps the most significant of these benefits is the investment potential of residential property. Information about current movements in house prices is exceedingly newsworthy. The figures collated by various building societies are regularly reported and news about price booms, in particular, often seems to be dealt with in a manner akin to news about pools' winners. There is a sense in which the home owner is seen as the lucky punter. In this particular game, however, most, if not all, the players get a prize. Over the course of the last two decades the underlying trend in house prices has outstripped the trends in retail prices, and expressed as rates of return they have exceeded those realised by many other investments. Putting one's money into housing is widely seen as being a safe, that is risk free, investment as well as offering returns generally higher than elsewhere. Indeed on the basis of aggregate trends, the reality of home ownership seems to bear out the perception, as analysis of the alternatives to house purchase show:

'Could an entrepreneur have done better elsewhere? Only someone with a very special combination of good fortune and personal characteristics could have expected to do so. Undoubtedly most could not. The average stock market speculator ... would not have done anywhere near as well.' (Farmer and Barrell 1981, p. 323)

There are, however, other attributes commonly ascribed to home ownership. For some the ownership of housing is an item of conspicuous consumption which confers status and identity on the individual. Short (1982) for example, has suggested that 'to become an owner occupier is a mark of success, while to remain a council tenant is considered an admission of failure' (p. 233) adding:

'It is not incidental that the first thing people do when they have bought their council house is to paint their door differently, add a bay window, change the facade and anything which establishes in the eyes of the outside world a new status for the inhabitants. People want to become owner-occupiers not only because it is financially beneficial; it is an indication of success, an emblem of higher status.' (p. 234)

These, widely-held views of home ownership are part of an 'ideology of tenures' (Harloe 1985, p. xxiii) in which the superiority of home ownership, over renting, is stressed. This superiority is not simply in the attributes of the tenure itself but also in the changes it produces in people's thoughts and actions. Tenure is seen as an independent variable, 'almost automatically, producing distinctive forms of thought, behaviour and actions' (Merrett 1982, p. 267). This can be recognised in, for example, the view that:

'Home-owners tend to be more prepared to pay for the upkeep and maintenance of their properties, since they have a financial interest in maintaining or increasing a home's capital value; tenants do not. The condition of the housing stock is therefore more likely to be maintained with owner occupation than with renting.' (Yates 1982, p. 218)

The distinctiveness of the positions of owners and of tenants has also formed the basis of discussions about the theoretical significance of home ownership: discussions in which the work of Peter Saunders has been central. He has argued that home ownership is a form of tenure which brings real material gains. These material gains, in the form of house prices, give home owners a distinctive common position since 'the objective interests of each individual owner-occupier are in maintaining and enhancing his material advantages and opportunities for realising capital gains through inflation of house market values' (Saunders, 1977, p. 14). These objective interests are, it is argued, different from those of tenants so that they form the foundation stones of housing classes. More recently Saunders (1984) has argued that the 'ownership of key means of consumption such as housing' have had the effect of creating 'a new major fault line in British society' (p. 203). His argument is that these 'consumption cleavages' may 'come to outweigh class alignments in respect of production, and that housing tenure remains the most important single aspect of such alignments because of the accumulative potential of house ownership' (p. 203). His thesis is, further, that such cleavages are being intensified by the privatization of welfare which has seen many areas of the welfare state turned over to market provision.

Politicians of both the Left and the Right, along with the drafters of government papers, have also stressed these same benefits of home ownership, as well as adding others of their own. 'Independence', 'freedom of choice', 'self reliance', 'security of tenure' are all seen to add up to a free, stable society in the shape of the 'property owning democracy'.

The Labour government's paper on the review of housing policy, for example, concluded that:

> 'A preference for home ownership is sometimes explained on the grounds that potential home owners believe that it will bring them financial advantage. A far more likely reason for the secular trend towards home ownership is the sense of greater personal independence that it brings. For most people owning one's own home is a basic and natural desire.' (DOE 1977, p. 50)

This view has entered into the political rhetoric of government housing policy as justification for widening the opportunities for home ownership. For example, the Secretary of State for the Environment argued when, in 1979, the House of Commons was debating the Housing Bill that:

> '.... this dramatic change in property values has opened up a division in the nation between those who own their own homes and those who do not. The further prices advanced the further the tenant fell behind ... Yesterday the Leader of the Opposition accused my party of encouraging a division in society. He conveniently omitted any reference to the greatest division of them all. And it is this division in the area of housing to which, in part, our legislation this Session will address itself.' (Hansard 17 June 1979, col. 409)

The belief that home ownership inexorably means benefits for the owner has had profound implications in the area of government policy. Housing policy has become dominated by the tenure issue. The widely prevailing view is that because home ownership offers so many benefits government should increase the opportunities for access to the tenure. Electorally this has proved popular, with many observers concluding that the 'right to buy' promise in the 1979 Conservative manifesto tipped the general election of that year in the

Conservatives' favour (Jacobs 1981). Subsequently the issue of council house sales has been of major ideological significance for the Left (see, for example, Griffiths and Holmes 1984), with the conflict being resolved by a firm, stated commitment by Labour to the continuation of sales. For the Conservatives, the support for home ownership remains as strong as ever. In their manifesto for the 1987 election this support was firmly stated:

'Nowhere has the spread of ownership been more significant than in housing. Buying their own home is the first step most people take towards building up capital to hand down to their children and grand children ...

'Home ownership has been the great success story of housing policy in the last eight years.

'Two out of every three homes are now owned by the people who live in them. This is a very high proportion, one of the largest in the world. We are determined to make it larger still.

'Some people are still deterred by the costs and complications of house purchase. That is why we must look for new ways to make house-buying simpler and easier.' (Conservative Party 1987)

The growing political support for home ownership has been consistent with a wider shift in British politics, based intellectually on the work of writers such as Hayek and Friedman, in which the freedom of the individual has been stressed. The teachings of the New Right have been extensively discussed elsewhere (see Bosanquet 1983; Mishra 1984). Both stress that the views of the various proponents are more diverse than commonly believed, but they can be crudely summarised as the belief that competitive markets are good, because they offer freedom, and state intervention is bad, because it does not. At the heart of this is the view that in order for society to advance and to be liberating, people must have as much freedom as possible to pursue their interests, and that, generally, coercion by the state interferes with that freedom. Notions of income equality are rejected, in part, because their achievement would involve the coercion by the state of some individuals to give up their privileges. Left to itself Adam Smith's 'hidden-hand' – the ability of the market to coordinate individuals' self interest – will produce outcomes which are those which individual members of the population prefer, and so maximize welfare in society.

The Conservative governments elected in 1979, 1983 and 1987 have been seeking ways of establishing this freedom by introducing market mechanisms to areas of activity which have long been deemed appropriately lodged with the state. The privatisation of nationalized industries, such as British Gas and

British Telecom, has been matched in housing by a switching of responsibility from local authorities to the market. As with other markets the common view is that the provision of housing through a market will ensure that people have the right to decide how much and what type of housing to consume. The sale of council houses and the promotion of home ownership, generally, are thus features of a wider trend to place more reliance on private markets.

The diversity of experience

The common view of home ownership, then, is that it offers benefits to the home owner. These benefits are many and are not available to the tenant. Such assertions have formed the basis of both government housing policy – fuelling and justifying the expansion of home ownership so that more can enjoy its benefits – and of theoretical discussions about the significance of tenure in establishing divisions within society.

The focus of this book is on empirical questions about the factual bases which inform both policy and theory. The importance of establishing this with respect to the latter has been argued, strongly, by Saunders:

> 'There is in the urban studies field today a growing recognition that theoretical debate and conjecture has run far ahead of empirical knowledge and historical understanding. The now substantial literature on the economic, political and sociological significance of home ownership is a case in point, for the long-running debate over housing tenure and social class (which in Britain can be traced back to the work of Rex and Moore in the 1960s) seems to have reached an inconclusive and somewhat unsatisfactory statement. Different theoretical positions have become enhanced while sound empirical and historical material which could be used to evaluate these positions and to drive the debate forward has been sadly lacking.' (Saunders 1986, p. 68)

The position taken here is that the empirical knowledge needs to be focussed on the diversity of experience of home owners. The focus is not on whether there are benefits of home ownership but on whether those benefits are universally enjoyed by home owners. The existence of such diversity would form a basis for critiques of established beliefs about the theoretical significance of home ownership and about the nature of outcomes in the market for home ownership.

The diversity of the impacts of home ownership has, in fact, already received some attention. Whitehead (1979), for example, in a perceptive paper, examined the widely held notion that home owners necessarily benefit from being able

5

to exercise freedom of choice over the home they choose to buy, how often to move, how much to pay and how much repairs and maintenance to carry out. Her argument is that in any market 'the benefits arising from choice depend on capacity to pay' (Whitehead 1979, p. 35). Going on to compare the position of local authority tenants with home owners she concluded that the latter do not always get the better deal:

> 'as far as choice is concerned, many of the so-called benefits of owner occupation depend on wealth and secure income rather than home ownership as such. All in all, being a poor owner-occupier may well be worse, in many respects, than being a council tenant.' (Whitehead 1979, p. 36)

In fact there exists a number of studies dating from the 1970s which provides empirical evidence to support contentions about the variation in the benefits which accrue to home owners. The work of Karn et al (1985), much of the empirical base of which is now a decade old, establishes that home ownership in parts of inner city Birmingham has been very different from the traditional image of home ownership. The owners interviewed had experienced difficulties in getting loans and problems in repaying them, and the properties they lived in were frequently in a condition which was 'beyond the resources of buyers to remedy' (p. 105). Moreover, the investment performance of their housing was poorer than comparable housing elsewhere. Other work by Karn (1979), the empirical base of which is even older, threw light on the phenomena of mortgage arrears and evictions following from mortgage possession actions amongst lower income buyers in Birmingham. Earlier Dennis (1970) had concluded of home owners in the slum clearance areas in Sunderland which he had studied that 'some of the normal advantages [of home ownership] are inoperative' (p. 236).

The publication of reports impugning the benefits of home ownership was, from the point of view of their date of publication, neither accidental nor without foundation. Indeed, the starting point of the empirical exploration reported in this book is that, in so far as the experience of home ownership has been one of various states of 'goodness', this has been the consequence of the fact that home owners were, by and large, the more prosperous members of society. That is, in Britain the experience of the home owner before the mid 1970s was usually a good one because their generally higher incomes enabled them to purchase that experience. As the performance of the national economy deteriorated, so did the fortunes of some home owners. There has been an historical association, therefore, between income and tenure which has obscured the real foundation of the home owner's experiences. In the remainder of this Chapter the changing nature of this historical association is briefly mapped out.

The changing face of the home owner

Over the course of the last 80 years there have been major changes in the ways in which we, in Britain, house ourselves. At the outset of the century the production and allocation of housing was based on market mechanisms. Renting 'from private landlords was seen as the normal means of obtaining somewhere to live' (Kemp 1987, p. 4) even for many of those with the financial means to buy. Public bodies provided a few thousand homes over the country as a whole, but private landlords provided about 90 per cent of homes with the remainder owned, and lived in, by private individuals. Since that time there have been long term and fundamental changes in the nature of housing provision. The private landlord has declined in significance whilst the public landlord has risen to a major position in the housing system. The most significant change, however, has arguably been the growing dominance of home ownership.

For the period from the 1920s until the 1970s the growth of home ownership occurred in a context of a national economy which meant higher and more stable real incomes for increasing numbers of the population. Any shift in preferences brought about by the shifting of the costs and benefits of the different housing tenures was backed up by the ability of increasing numbers of the population to meet the long-term financial commitment of home ownership. From the start of this period there were increasing numbers of people working in non-manual and professional occupations who were immune from the widespread practice of employment by the day and even by the hour which had characterized the working life of so many in the nineteenth century. For many, home ownership appeared a desirable solution to their housing needs and by 1938 the sector had increased its share of the housing stock from 10 per cent to 32 per cent largely by recruiting from the new middle classes. Thus Bowley (1945) noted from one survey that of the manual and lower paid non-manual workers living in urban areas 17.8 per cent were home owners, and from another survey that of civil servants, local government officials and teachers 64.7 per cent were home owners. Although there was widespread unemployment during the 1930s it has been argued that unemployment was primarily experienced by tenants so that the new home owners were not so adversely affected by the prevailing economic changes (Doling et al 1986).

Although the conditions of the immediate post war years were not conducive to further increases, by the 1950s the economic environment again fuelled demand for home ownership. There was a general shortage of labour in most parts of the country. More and more sectors of the population including those in manual occupations enjoyed relatively high wages and stable employment. Over the course of the following quarter of a century the continued expansion of home ownership meant that the tenure ceased to be mainly the preserve of the white collar worker. Increasingly skilled, semi-skilled and even unskilled workers were buying their own homes. By the mid 1970s a fifth of unskilled manual workers and a third of semi-skilled and personal service workers were home owners (see Table 1.1). Indeed, even at this time, home ownership was 'much more of a mixed tenure in terms of occupation than [was] renting from public authorities' (DOE 1977, p. 84).

Table 1.1 Home Ownership by Occupational Type, Great Britain 1976

Occupational type	Proportion who are:	
	outright owner %	with mortgage %
Professional	25	66
Employers/Managers	34	48
Intermediate non-manual	28	44
Junior non-manual	30	26
Skilled manual and own account non-manual	19	29
Semi-skilled & personal service	18	15
Unskilled manual	16	5

Source: General Household Survey

If, by the mid-1970s the socio-economic profile of home owners had shifted, subsequent trends have led to further changes. Whilst the growth of home ownership in the 30 years up to 1980 was steady and continuous, since 1980 there has been a quickening of the pace. The Housing Act of that year gave most local authority, and some housing association tenants a statutory right to buy their homes with the aid of large discounts on market values. In addition, the government has used its control over local finance both to increase council house rents and to prevent large scale additions to the local authority stock. In numerical terms the results have been dramatic. In England in 1969 50.9 per cent of households were home owners and 27.8 per cent local authority tenants. Ten years later, in 1979, 56.5 per cent were home owners and 29.6 per cent local authority tenants. In the following five years, however, the trajectories of the two tenures diverged: the home owner sector increased rapidly to 62.9 per cent whereas the local authority sector, for the first time since 1919, declined in size to 25.6 per cent.

Rapid expansion of home ownership has been possible by the entry of many more from those groups with lower incomes, and so the degree of heterogeneity within home ownership has become even more marked. In addition, the last decade has been one in which there have been large scale changes in the labour market. One of the results has been that large numbers of both tenants and home owners have experienced unemployment. Not infrequently the unemployment has been long term, rather than a transient stage between jobs, and, for many, household incomes have fallen considerably. The changes have not stopped there, however. Recently there have been other developments in both the demand and supply sides of the home owner market – increasing numbers of retired households and an aging housing stock, for example. These have had the effect of creating increasing numbers of owners with low incomes for whom the financial commitments of owning have sometimes weighed heavy. They have also had the effect of creating outcomes which are often unlike the outcomes normally associated with home ownership.

This book, therefore, centres around an argument that our perceptions of home ownership have been locked into a model based on the 1960s and 1970s when the majority of home owners were sharing the benefits of an expanding economy characterised by full-employment. The pervasive image of the comfortable, well-maintained, suburban semi which gave home owners advantages over tenants may no longer be relevant. Many home owners do not share the economic prosperity on which such images are based.

In writing this book it is not our intention to 'bash' or discredit home ownership as a tenure. Rather it is the extent to which the traditional image of home ownership, as a set of desirable attributes such as independence, choice, status and so on matches up with the present day reality of many people's experiences of the tenure which this book seeks to explore. What are the consequences of combining home ownership with low incomes? To what extent have other trends such as unemployment and demographic changes contributed to these consequences? To what extent does the market deliver the goods?

The plan of this book

Much of our systematic information about home ownership and home owners is based on statistical data which are aggregated to national and, sometimes, regional levels. Whereas this provides much enlightenment, arithmetic means and one-way distributions disguise a great deal. They disguise, particularly, when the object of concern is diversity and how that diversity relates to other variables and trends. What much of existing data – about house price trends, for example – tell us is obscured by the level of aggregation such that we can discern relationships about the norm or average but not, generally, about divergences from that average. The identification of the picture we wish to examine is obscured further by the fact that the housing market is not a national one. The nature of supply and demand may vary so considerably from one part of the country to another that it is more appropriate to consider the existence of geographically discrete housing markets which have considerable independence from one another. Indeed even within a single geographical area we can begin by conceding the possibility of relatively independent 'sub markets'. One consequence is that our need for information will not be met by national and regional data alone: local data are also required. To the latter end, research about the housing market in Coventry supplies evidence of diversity appropriate for the present book. Each of the Chapters of this book, therefore, presents evidence at each of the different levels of aggregation to reveal something about the diversity at and between each level – national, regional, local and sub-market.

Chapter 2 considers the rationale for examining data at these different levels of aggregation. It also discusses the appropriateness of selecting Coventry as the basis for information about local housing markets. No single part of the country could be representative of the rest of the country. Indeed, as we have argued, it is part of our intention to demonstrate local diversity. It follows that it is not possible to claim that Coventry is typical of the rest of the country or of anywhere else. Indeed, if our discussions about the localness of housing markets are sustainable the claim could not be made of any single locality. To that extent many different local housing markets would be suitable objects of empirical investigation though Coventry is particularly appropriate by virtue of its juxtaposition of a high rate of home ownership and a high rate of unemployment.

In Chapter 3 data at various levels of aggregation are used to demonstrate trends, and variations, in the supply and demand for home ownership. Specifically, it indicates the existence of a growing band of home owners who are located in the lower half of the income distribution. A distinction is also made between those who have low incomes when they enter home ownership, and those whose incomes fall after entry. For the latter group some consideration is given to the way in which their financial room for manoeuvre is structured by the nature of home ownership and the specific means by which it is purchased. One message of this Chapter is that the market for home ownership has distinctive characteristics and these heavily influence the link between trends in demand and market outcomes.

The subsequent three Chapters each examine a different phenomenon of home ownership – mortgage arrears, physical condition and price trends. The intention in each is to demonstrate that not only are there large variations

10

between home owners, but that getting into home ownership is not necessarily achieving a great success. The nature of the market is such that all home owners do not necessarily achieve great freedom, great status, great security or great capital growth. There is, in other words, both good and bad home ownership. Although in these Chapters there is an emphasis on the effect of unemployment in achieving this diversity, this emphasis is not exclusive. We also attempt to demonstrate the impacts of the juxatposition of home ownership and low income generally, of the nature of housing markets, and of government policy. If these additions are desirable because they widen the analysis they are also, to an extent, necessary because of the methodological difficulties in separating them out.

In the final Chapter an attempt is made to bring together the main findings of earlier Chapters. It also indicates the nature of some of the conclusions of these findings. What do they have to say about the nature and meaning of home ownership? What sort of equality and freedom is obtained through market provision? What do they say for the future of home ownership?

2 Setting the scene

The purpose of this Chapter is to discuss some preliminary aspects of the empirical work on which this book is based. It examines, firstly, the issue of the appropriate level of aggregation at which to consider the nature and experience of home ownership. Secondly, a brief economic and housing history of Coventry is provided to give the reader a background to the particular market conditions which prevail there. Finally, the selection and nature of the smaller, study areas within Coventry is discussed.

The scale of analysis

Despite reference to 'the housing market' and the 'British housing system', housing markets are not national. It is true that national factors are important in setting parameters in which housing outcomes are decided. Inflation, interest rates, housing subsidies and the planning system are phenomena which are nationwide in their impact, and influence both supply and demand. But housing markets are essentially local. This point has been made by McAvinchey and Maclennan (1982) whose analysis of house price changes at the regional scale 'makes quite apparent the heterogeneity of the housing market across the British regions' (p. 53). Their emphasis on the region should not, however, be taken as meaning that the region is necessarily the appropriate level of analysis for our purposes, other than that being the smallest spatial unit for which house price data are commonly available (see Chapter 6). More appropriate, since the local labour market is an important determinant of demand, might be the travel to work area (TTWA).

To develop that suggestion it is useful to start from considerations of the household sector and the processes by which, in a very general sense, individual households are distributed throughout the housing stock. Some households contain no members who are actually or potentially active in the labour market. Other households may contain more than one such individual. Each of the households in a TTWA, however, operates within the housing system and, with the exception of a small proportion who are without a roof over their heads, distribute themselves throughout the housing stock. The results of this distribution are far from even. This follows in the first place from the fact that the housing stock itself is internally differentiated with each dwelling having a different set of characteristics: different construction types, quality, size, number of rooms, and location with respect to other households, land uses and activities. The housing system is also differentiated with respect to tenure. Over the country as a whole the largest tenure is home ownership divided about equally between outright owners and those with mortgages, with the remaining dwellings being owned by a variety of public and private landlords.

Nationally in excess of two thirds of all dwellings, each made up of a unique combination of characteristics, are distributed amongst households through market mechanisms. Who gets what is, in other words, essentially controlled by the price system rather than bureaucratic rules. The income of the consumer is, however, arguably more crucial in the housing market than in many other markets. This arises because there are three factors which make the cost of purchasing legal rights over housing persistently high in relation to average income. Firstly, and nothwithstanding any metaphysical debates, housing in our society is a necessity regardless of income in the sense that a 'normal' life style is dependent upon access to certain sorts of physical structure. Secondly, there are some legal limits on the minimum amounts and quality of housing which must be paid for: repair notices, for example, may be served on owners of housing in substantial disrepair. Thirdly, the benefits derived from housing can go beyond those of physical suitability to include status, independence, and investment. In general, competition for desirable housing is intense. For many, housing expenditure accounts for a major share of their budget and is their costliest single purchase. Some cannot afford even the minimum amount without assistance from the State or elsewhere.

These various aspects of the market in housing mean that there is a particularly obvious connection with the labour market. In general terms those people with higher paid jobs can exercise more spending power in the housing market, and indeed in other markets. The correlation is not perfect: intergenerational transfers of property and other forms of wealth are one complication, the number of dependents, and expected future income others. Nevertheless in broad terms there is a sifting of households, in this market

13

for high-priced 'necessities', on the basis of the household's position in the labour market. In a very real sense what you live in depends on what you do in the labour market.

There are also locational aspects to this relationship. Houses are spatially fixed, and although it is not invariably the case, so are jobs. Physical, financial and other factors place limits on the extent to which the two can be separated. Tolerance to commuting will vary over time and between different households and cultures, but in aggregate, and around large conglomerations of jobs, there will be travel to work areas in which households are operating for both their work and housing needs. The interrelationship has been summarized in the following way:

> 'From the point of view of the individual worker, the location of his residence also limits his choice of job. The locations of job opportunities and of places of residence are mutually linked in space by the commuting "tolerances" of workers. Given the location of workplaces in centralised nodes, the area over which housing opportunities will be sought by a household depends on its members' tolerance to commuting. In the same way, given the location of residence, the workers in a household seek employment opportunities over an area defined in terms of commuting tolerance' (Johnson, Salt and Wood 1973, p. 28).

The locational aspect may, however, also operate in the opposite direction. It may be the case as Macgregor (1977), for example, has argued that the position of the household in the labour market is dependent to an extent on their position in the housing market. This may arise when the stereotype image of certain residential areas leads potential employers not to offer jobs to the residents of those areas.

There are levels below the journey to work area which are important analytically, however. Indeed in a sense the individual house is the appropriate level of analysis. This is because a feature of residential dwellings, whether owner occupied or rented, is their complexity. In itself this is not unique since many other commodities, such as cars and foreign holidays, are also multidimensional. What is perhaps different is the degree of complexity which goes beyond physical characteristics. Ingram and Oron (1977) have posited that the benefits which occupiers receive from a dwelling are derived from three distinct characteristics of the dwelling. Firstly, there is the physical structure itself which is of a certain size, on a plot of a given size, divided into rooms with an interior finish and mechanical subsystems, such as central heating, of a certain quality. Secondly, there is the type and quality of the neighbourhood. Thirdly, houses are also differentiated by accessibility to local public goods, such as schools and open space, to other people and to other

14

land uses. Each dwelling consists of a combination of these three characteristics which together define the services which can be derived from it. This level of complexity combines with another characteristic of housing – its spatial fixity – to result in the uniqueness of each house. Even apartments in the same building may be differentiated by which side of the building they are on and floor level. As commodities therefore, they are not perfect substitutes.

However, clearly some houses are closer substitutes than others. Neighbouring houses of the same size and layout in the same terrace will be closer substitutes to each other than either will be to a larger, detached house located some distance away. In these circumstances it is tempting to think in terms of sub-markets within each of which the main housing characteristics including location, are broadly similar. Indeed, although we do not provide a more formal definition of sub-markets, it is this notion of similarity which forms the basis of the use of the term in this book. Notwithstanding the partly common-sense basis for this notion of sub-markets, it is worth noting that Maclennan (1982) has made the point that substitutability, in the way referred to here, may be too weak a definition of housing sub-markets, and that a stronger definition would be that price per unit of housing service varied over space or over quality. His studies in Glasgow and Aberdeen suggest that small areas of similar housing can show quite different rates of house price inflation in both the short and long term. This lends some credence to our definition.

What we have indicated here, then, is that an empirical examination of the diversity of home ownership and of whether home ownership is matching up to its traditional image cannot rely entirely on data aggregated to the national level. Although such data can tell us something about home ownership they can also disguise the range of experiences. Depending upon the relative dominance of local over national factors it is quite possible for households in some regions, travel to work areas or sub markets to have quite different experiences to households in other regions, travel to work areas or sub markets. Home owners in the South East, for example, might be experiencing high rates of house price increase whilst those in the North West do not; or whilst they are increasing in the South East generally, the experience in some sub markets might be that they are declining.

In the light of these considerations the data used here relate to a number of geographical levels. Firstly, there are published data sources – such as the English House Condition Surveys – which provide information about national and regional trends. Some other published literature also provides national and regional information. These sources enable some broad conclusions to be drawn about the heterogeneity of the sector. Secondly, some data have been obtained for the city of Coventry. Although the city boundary does not coincide with the TTWA, Coventry is at least a fairly large urban area separated, geographically, from other urban areas. This means that the city does incorporate the central core of the

15

TTWA, so that many influences will be constant over its housing market. Thirdly, a number of 'sub markets' have been studied in depth in order to examine the individual experiences of home owners at different levels in the market.

Coventry: The economic and housing sectors

As a forerunner to the discussion of the identification of 'sub markets' and the data collected, this section provides a brief history of Coventry which stresses the interplay between the local economy and the developing housing market. Some of the major differences between Coventry and the rest of the country, in so far as these may be pertinent to an understanding of the differences in people's experiences of home ownership, are also identified.

Although throughout the course of the present century Coventry's employment base has been, at any one time, quite narrowly focussed on a small number of industries, until recently those industries were ones which were expanding more rapidly than others. Even before the onset of this century, the invention of the safety bicycle (in 1884) and the patenting of the pneumatic tyre (in 1889) was followed by a growing demand for bicycles which were made in Coventry's factories. The boom lasted well into this century, but before it began to wane Coventry experienced an expansion in motor cycle output. By 1905 there were already 22 motor cycle manufacturers in the city (Richardson 1972). During the same period motor car production also established itself in Coventry. Responding to growing consumer demand these industries, together with allied engineering industries, took on more workers. High wages attracted a large influx of migrants to Coventry the population of which grew from 69,978 in 1901 to 119,003 in 1914. Coventry took on 'the klondike atmosphere of a boom town of high earnings, housing shortage, over-crowding, [and] militant trade unionism' (Hodgkinson 1970, p. 2).

The same pattern continued during the inter war period. Whilst most of the country endured deep economic depression, Coventry experienced an extraordinary period of economic and population expansion. The motor vehicle and engineering firms operating in the city offered high wages so that Coventry workers were comparatively well off; in 1938 the ownership of cars in the city was 68 per 1000 population compared with 39 per 1000 elsewhere (Richardson 1972). Migrants continued to flock into the city with the result that by 1939 its population had reached 220,000.

The rapid increase in population clearly meant a rapid increase in housing need. Following the Addison Act of 1919, the local authority had powers to meet this need but 'for many years the city failed to meet the government quota on housing' (Lancaster 1985, p. 8). Between 1919 and 1939, 28 per cent

16

of all dwellings built in England and Wales were council built: the corresponding figure for Coventry was 13 per cent. The main thrust of the Council's strategy was to provide active encouragement to private builders. This was done by purchasing a large piece of land to the south of the city, which was then cleared, sub-divided and sold to speculative builders. An important factor underlying the viability of this strategy was that although Coventry had relatively few middle class inhabitants it 'did have during the 1930s the more prosperous workers in Britain' (Lancaster 1985, p. 9). One of the consequences was that the demand for home ownership was buoyant: 'At first the builders were surprised to find factory workers scanning the new estates in search of housing and willing to buy rather than to rent' (Lancaster 1985, p. 9). The result was that 'by the late 1930's [Coventry] had one of the highest rates of working class home ownership in Britain' (Lancaster 1985, p. 9).

After the Second World War the Coventry economy continued to expand. Its war factories were re-equipped to produce both aircraft and motor vehicles. Together with its other manufacturing industries – in tractors, motor cycles, electrical engineering – production increased to meet the increasing demand from not only the home market but also the export market where, because of war damage on the Continent, there were few European competitors. The increase in the labour demands of these industries again resulted in large numbers of people flocking in from elsewhere. By 1961 the population had reached 305,521. The nature of the labour demands, however, ensured that this population was strongly slanted in terms of its social class composition. In 1951 68.4 per cent of the workforce was employed in the manufacturing sector and amongst these there were proportionately more skilled workers than elsewhere in the country. The corollary was that there were relatively few people employed in the service sector, and relatively few in professional and managerial occupations. The growth of Coventry, then, has been the rise of a high-waged, skilled working class.

The continuing influx of newcomers to Coventry, together with the growth of the existing population, imposed pressures on the housing system to which both the public and private sectors responded. In comparison with the rest of the country, however, council housing took a smaller role. Although the production of council housing followed the same general pattern as at national level, in Coventry the peaks were shorter and the slumps lower and longer. Thus over the 30 years between 1951 and 1980 Coventry's local authority house building programme bettered that of England and Wales as a proportion of all house building in only seven years (1951, 1953, 1966–1969 and 1970) and was equal to it for two. One explanation suggested for this relatively lower level of local authority house building was the 'massive reconstruction needed in the City Centre after the war' (CDP 1970, p. 69). The result was that in housing private developers took the major initiative.

17

The mid–1960s was, in many important respects, a watershed for Coventry. Production in its principal industry, car assembly, peaked in 1964 and two years later total employment in Coventry peaked. In subsequent years the local economy declined. In this Coventry was not unique; similar processes were operating at the national level. During the late 1960s the national economy was characterized by high rates of inflation and interest, low rates of economic growth and the loss of export markets. Throughout the country sections of manufacturing industry were also undergoing reorganization and rationalization. Mergers and internal changes affected capital investment decisions and the location of productive capacity. In 1966 manufacturing industries in Coventry had accounted for 63.3 per cent of all employment but over the following 15 years, and particularly between 1976 and 1981, this fell to 46.6 per cent. This was not a reflection of the inability of the local economy to generate new enterprise, but rather a change in the willingness of surviving establishments to maintain previously existing employment levels (Healey and Clark 1984). Thus of the 52,908 jobs lost from 1974 to 1982, 80 per cent were lost by the fifteen largest manufacturing firms. These included British Leyland (workforce reduced from 27,258 to 8,221), Talbot (12,537 to 6,900), GEC (16,166 to 10,464), Tooling Investments (5,469 to 798), Massey Ferguson (6,014 to 4,543), Dunlop (5,749 to 3,413) and Associated Engineering (2,679 to 1,035).

Although in proportionate (and absolute) terms the service sector is now more important – service employment increased from 64,748 in 1971 to 73,460 in 1981 and from 33.1 per cent to 50.2 per cent of total employment – Coventry remains essentially a working class town in which the active workforce is dominated by both manual and low paid, non-manual employment.

The changing fortunes of Coventry's labour market have been associated with other changes – in unemployment, in population and in earnings. Although the level of unemployment in Coventry fluctuated throughout the post war period, up to 1966 it was relatively low, around the 1 per cent mark. It was therefore lower than the national figure of around 2 per cent. Since it has been argued (Paish 1962) that 2 per cent would mainly include people who were 'unemployable' or in the process of changing jobs, the Coventry figure demonstrated a considerable labour shortage problem. This created distortions in the local labour market: many firms did not lay off workers during slumps, for example, because of fears of not being able to recruit labour during booms (City of Coventry 1963). After 1966 unemployment continued to fluctuate but the underlying trend turned upwards. In 1967 the unemployment rate in the Coventry travel to work area exceeded that of the country as a whole, the positions reversing in 1969. Reversing again in 1971, and with the exception of 1973, the Coventry rate has been higher than the national rate ever since.

The period 1966 to 1974 was thus a transitional one, since when, Coventry has been an unemployment blackspot.

Following the large increase in population after 1945 the rate of increase firstly slowed and then became negative. Between 1961 and 1971 there was for the first time in approximately one hundred years – with the exception of the Second World War – a large movement of people out of Coventry. Some of this out-migration was short-distanced as people searched for better and more suitable housing outside the city boundary. To that extent it was the continuation of the trend starting in the 1920s for the white collar and more affluent blue collar workers to move into Coventry's hinterland (Crossman 1970). From the mid–1960s, however, it also reflected the decline in employment opportunities within Coventry (Smith 1983). Indeed from 1971 to 1981 the net outward flow of migrants for the first time exceeded the balance of births over deaths.

Although there are many difficulties about using average earnings as an indicator of local prosperity they nevertheless seem to confirm the other changes occurring in Coventry. In the folklore of early post-war Britain, the West Midlands, in general, and Coventry, in particular, led the wages chart. Wage rates in Coventry were traditionally a target for workers in pay negotiations elsewhere in the country (IDS 1971). The differentials were, moreover, large. In the 1950s the Coventry rate was some one third higher than the wages received in the vehicle industries elsewhere in the country (Mallier and Rosser 1982). Similarly, DHSS statistics showed that in the second half of the 1960s male workers in Coventry, on average, earned about 13 to 14 per cent more than male workers elsewhere in the country. During the 1970s, however, Coventry's relative prosperity began to wane. It began the decade having average wages in excess of the average for the West Midlands conurbation as a whole, which in turn had wages higher than the national average. Since then their position on the wages ladder has slipped from relative prosperity to relative poverty. It should be noted, that these averages exclude the unemployed so that they represent the average of those in work. The actual average for Coventry for all those of working age, would because of its high level of unemployment, be lower than the official statistics suggest.

The change in the structure of the labour market has been significant in another way, however. The lead in the wages table enjoyed by the West Midlands Region and Coventry prior to the early 1970s was almost entirely due to the large numbers employed in vehicles industries. In 1974 18 per cent of the West Midlands sample in the New Earnings Survey were employed in the vehicles order; by 1982 this had declined to 12 per cent (Smith 1984). So much of the reduction in the average wage level can be explained by the loss from the sample of this large and high waged industrial order. Indeed if the sample composition had not changed the decline would have been of minor proportions: 'In 1980, the old 1973 numbers would have put the West Midlands Region

19

well above the national average' (Smith 1984, p. 31). The changing fortunes of the Coventry labour force therefore reflect a variety of individual changes in which many have become worse off, some become better off, but many remaining at the same relative position.

The study areas

Whilst Coventry, as a whole, has undergone large changes in its prosperity the impact has not been the same for everyone, nor in all its areas. In order to examine these differences eight 'sub markets' or study areas have been identified on the basis of a number of criteria.

Firstly, the areas had to be representative of different sectors of the home ownership market in Coventry. This would enable an examination of the heterogeneity of the tenure. Secondly, it was necessary for the main supply side factors – house type, size and accessibility to parks, transport facilities and so on – to be roughly constant for each area. This requirement also meant that each area could not be so large that there were internal variations arising from locational differences. On these bases eight areas were selected, with two areas each representing four 'rungs' on the housing ladder. These did not include the very cheapest nor the most expensive rungs since these were not found to be clustered, geographically except where there was considerable variation in house type. The more expensive areas, in particular, were characterized by their lack of uniformity. In addition, by limiting the study to the built up area within the boundaries of the local authority many other parts of the housing market in which Coventry commuters bought homes were excluded. This also meant much up-market housing. Although the eight study areas are representative of rungs on the housing ladder, therefore, they are by no means representative of the whole ladder. Rather, they are concentrated at the middle and lower ends. For the purposes of the discussion in later Chapters, however, the terms 'upper' and 'top' will be used to refer to those areas of our eight which are most up-market, and 'lower' or 'bottom' to those most down-market.

The location of the eight areas varied from inner city to the periphery of the city (see Figure 2.1). In the two most expensive areas – Mount Nod and Allesley Park – the market value in 1985 of a three bedroomed, semi-detached house with a garage – was almost £30,000. Both areas were developed about 1960, contain a number of open, green spaces and a mixture of house types, which are mostly occupied by home owners. In 1981 relatively few of its residents were unemployed or retired. The two least expensive areas – Hillfields and Charterhouse were developed before World War One largely with two and three bedroomed terraced houses, most of which have been subsequently

20

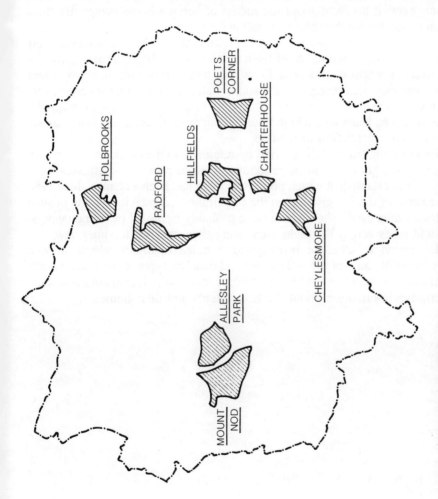

Figure 2.1 The Location of the Eight Study Areas

improved. Frequently this has involved converting the third bedroom into a bathroom. Such a house cost about £11,000 in 1985. Its residents were more likely than in other parts of Coventry to be outside employment by virtue of unemployment or retirement. Table 2.1 shows the intermediate 'rungs', and the similarity in the characteristics of Cheylesmore and Poets Corner, and of Radford and Holbrooks. Indeed, in many of the subsequent Tables the areas are grouped by their market position as 'Top' (Allesley Park and Mount Nod), 'Upper-middle' (Poets Corner and Cheylesmore), 'Lower-middle' (Radford and Holbrooks) and 'Bottom' (Charterhouse and Hillfields).

A household survey was carried out of recent buyers, that is households who had bought their present home during the five years prior to the survey. The reasons for this particular focus was that they would all have made a recent, explicit decision about the merits of being a home owner. By their action in purchasing they had demonstrated a preference (given the constraints facing them) for home ownership rather than renting. The recentness of their decision also separated them off from those who had been in their home for a protracted length of time and for whom home ownership may no longer be a conscious preference. It was, additionally, assumed that recent buyers as a group were more likely to be susceptible to financial stress – for example, many would be faced with a high financial outlay on housing and other family commitments in relation to income.

The sampling frame was selected by reference to the electoral register. In each of the eight study areas randomly selected sheets of addresses were examined to establish at which properties there had been a change since 1980 in the name of those registered on the electoral roll. Visual inspection of such addresses then established which were probably occupied by home owners. 306 addresses across the eight areas were then selected for interview.

The interview schedule investigated a range of topics which allowed exploration of some of the difficulties and disadvantages of the respondent's experience, in their present house, of home ownership. It also obtained some descriptive information about the respondents and their homes.

Table 2.1 Characterisics of the Study Areas

	Mount Nob	Allesley Park	Cheylesmore	Poets Corner	Radford	Holbrooks	Charterhouse	Hillfields	Coventry
% unemployed 1981	4.1	3.9	4.5	4.5	6.9	10.9	9.5	13.6	5.9
% retired 1981	5.6	5.1	11.5	13.1	10.9	9.5	12.1	10.5	9.4
% home owners 1981	97.5	92.4	89.3	91.4	74.1	66.3	67.1	52.6	66.4
% council housing 1981	0.5	1.5	4.5	2.3	10.1	21.6	16.7	13.7	22.9
Survey house - type	semi	semi	semi & terrace	terrace	terrace	terrace	terrace	terrace	-
- bedrooms	3	3	3	3	3	3	2	2	-
- 1985 price (£000)	29	29	23	20	17	13	11	11	-

Source: 1981 Census enumeration data; and Coventry House Price Survey

3 Supply of and demand for home ownership

In this Chapter we bring together evidence of certain characteristics of, and changes in, the supply and demand for home ownership. The concern is not with the growth of the sector – although as we indicate in Chapter one this has had consequences for the diversity of the sector – but rather our concern is with that diversity. The aim is to describe something of the evolving and diverse nature of the home owner, and of their homes. The first part of the Chapter contains evidence that, on the demand side, the amount and quality of housing which many groups of home owners are able to purchase and maintain has been influenced by trends which have differentially affected the incomes of home owners. On the supply side there have been other trends which have also resulted in increasing heterogeneity. In presenting these trends an attempt has been made to bring together, though not systematically, factual evidence at the following four levels of aggregation: national; regional; Coventry; and sub market. The finer level of disaggregation, in particular, demonstrates the differences within the home ownership sector. What these differences amount to is a growing number of low income home owners, facing prices which are high relative to average incomes. The final section of the Chapter considers a framework for thinking about the way in which, in these circumstances, home owners make expenditure decisions.

The changing face of demand

In considering the existence of home owners with low incomes a distinction can usefully be drawn between those who have low incomes when they enter home ownership, and those who suffer a reduction in income after they have entered. The former will include those people who are marginal, in a financial sense, to the tenure having an income which is small in relation to housing costs even at the cheaper end of the market. They are thus able to get their foot onto the bottom of the ladder, but only just so, and in the short term, at least, they might be financially more comfortable in a rental sector. The latter group will include those who have entered home ownership with a medium or even high income but whose income has then fallen. This fall may have been planned or at least anticipated as when someone has retired, either early or at the statutory age, or where a second income has been given up because of planned child rearing. In such cases the household has had the opportunity, which it may or may not have taken, to apply forethought to its financial position and to proceed in the knowledge that it can continue to meet its housing costs. There are, however, also some whose income drops after entry, but for reasons which are unexpected and unplanned. Redundancy, loss of overtime earnings, short time working, injury or sickness, marital breakdown, unplanned pregnancy, for example, might all result in loss of household income. In comparison with those whose income loss was planned, there may be a poor fit between existing financial commitments and the new level of income. The problem for the individuals concerned then comes of finding a strategy which brings expenditure and income more into line.

A further aspect of the distinction between those who have low incomes when they enter, and those who become low income earners after entry, into home ownership relates to the meaning of 'low'. In the case of the former group income can be interpreted as low in relation to the price of a house at the cheaper end of the market. Since average house prices vary from one part of the country to another, the figure which defines 'low' needs a spatial dimension. In the case of the latter group, however, the reduction in income might not take the household into the 'low' income band for a given area, though if their housing or other commitments are large their ability to match income and expenditure might nevertheless be difficult. Thus a household with two people each earning £20,000 per year and with a mortgage of £80,000, could lose one of their incomes with the result that they remain, by national standards, a high income household but with a mortgage commitment which would be difficult to sustain. It might be more accurate to say of this latter group, therefore, that they had 'lower' incomes than when they entered home ownership. A similar statement might be made about households with retired

25

heads: most of them will have lower incomes than when they worked, but it will depend what they are able to add to their state pension (in terms of investments, occupational pensions and so on) whether they also have 'low' incomes.

There has been little, if any, systematic study of the incidence and nature of low income home ownership at the national level. A study using a random sample survey of households in Birmingham carried out in 1976 did attempt to derive estimates of the numbers and types of low income home ownership at the local level, however (Doling 1983). At that time, the average price paid by a first time buyer in the West Midlands Region was about £9,000, and by first and subsequent buyers in Birmingham's inner city approximately £5-6,000. Taking a 'low' income to be £3,000 or under (they would have to borrow at least twice their income in order to purchase an inner city house), 36 per cent of all home owners fell into this category. Amongst these, households consisting of one or two persons over retirement age dominated, accounting for 62.3 per cent of the total, with households consisting of two adults plus one or more children accounting for a further 17.3 per cent. Single person and single parent households, under the age of 60-65 years were represented in this group more frequently than they were in the population of home owner households in general.

This same study also used other criteria to specify 'low' income households. The aim was to define low in relation to household needs with respect to both the size of the household and their mortgage outgoings. The method adopted was similar to that used in the definition of the poverty line (see Townsend 1979) where a low income was defined as being equal to the sum of mortgage costs plus the needs of the household as defined by the supplementary benefit scale rates which were increased by an arbitrary factor of 1.5. The results of the Birmingham exercise were not markedly different in terms of the proportion of home owners identified as having low incomes, though there was a greater incidence of large families.

Although this study suggests that there may have been a sizeable proportion of the home owner population whose incomes were in some sense low – perhaps over a third of all home owners – it was not able to provide much evidence of the ways in which they had reached that position. Moreover, given events since 1976 – increased unemployment and marital breakdown for example – it seems likely that the scale and nature of the phenomenon may have changed significantly. In the rest of this section evidence of some of these other trends is presented.

Unemployment

Perhaps the most significant of these trends has been large and rapid changes in the labour market. These are only approximately recorded by unemployment statistics not least because of periodic changes in definitions but also because they do not always count losses of second and subsequent incomes within households and do not record at all short time working, loss of overtime earnings and business failure. Even so, the statistics are useful for showing the broad trends in unemployment. Figure 3.1 shows that nationally from a low level in the mid–60s unemployment has increased in a number of steps but rising particularly rapidly from 1979–1982. In part, this rise in unemployment has resulted from an increase in the working population – defined as the sum of the employed labour force and the unemployed. Thus over the period 1965 to 1985 the working population increased by 1.3 million. But the number of jobs, and thus the employed labour force, decreased by 1.2 million, with most of this decrease occurring since 1980.

For present purposes it is important to look at where these job losses occurred and which sorts of worker have been involved. The key to these enquiries lies in the fact that manufacturing industry has been the main source of job losses. In Great Britain as a whole the number of people employed in the service sector actually increased over the period 1980 to 1984 by 0.7 per cent. Over the same period jobs in manufacturing industry decreased by 18.7 per cent. But the decrease has not been constant throughout the manufacturing sector with the largest losses, in absolute terms, occurring in metal manufacturing, engineering, and vehicles. Thus over the period from 1967 to 1983 there were 3.3 million jobs lost in all manufacturing orders, with 1.5 millions of those in the 4 orders specified. The corresponding losses for the 1979 to 1983 period alone are 1.7 million and 0.8 million.

It follows from these broad features of job loss that much of the unemployment of recent years has occurred amongst those occupational groups which form the bulk of the labour force in the manufacturing sector. That is amongst manual workers of the skilled, semi-skilled and unskilled categories. But unemployment has also had a marked regional dimension with those parts of the country which were traditionally manufacturing centres, particularly in the metal, engineering and vehicles sectors, having experienced the greatest job losses. So not only has the manufacturing sector declined least in the South East, South West and East Anglia, because they contained less of this type of manufacturing, but generally they have had a smaller proportion of their workforce in manufacturing to begin with. There has also been a regional dimension to changes in the service sector, which too has increased most in the South East, South West and East Anglia. The overall result is that unemployment rates reflect this north-south divide, with rates being far lower in the south (see Table 3.1).

Although there has been a marked industrial and regional dimension to unemployment most sectors of society have not escaped. The DHSS cohort study, for example, found that nationally over one third of unemployed householders were home owners and one fifth had mortgages (DHSS 1984).

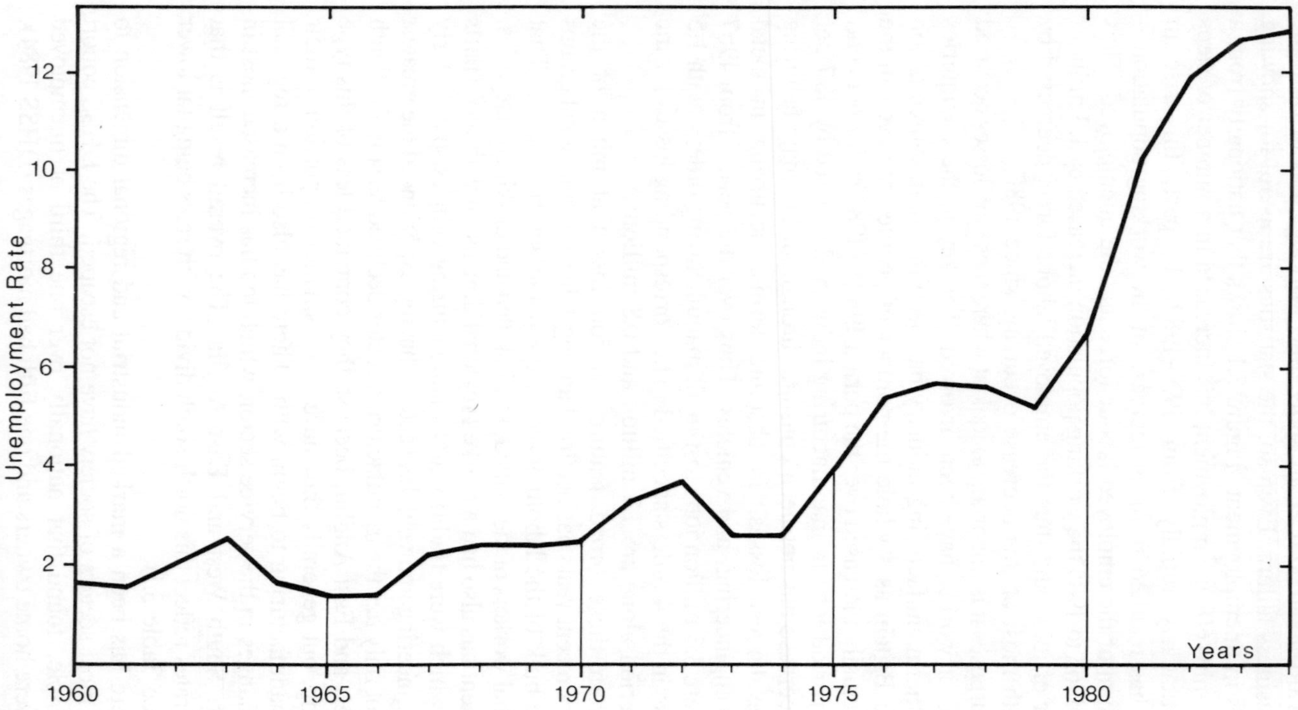

Years

1980

1975

1970

1965

1960

Unemployment Rate

12

10

8

6

4

2

Source: CSO, Annual Abstract of Statistics, various

Figure 3.1 Unemployment Rate, Great Britain, 1960-1984

28

Table 3.1 Unemployment (June 1985)

(Percentage)

Region	Unemployed			Unemployed excluding school leavers Seasonally adjusted
	All	Male	Female	All
South East	9.6	11.4	7.2	9.7
Greater London[a]	10.3	12.3	7.4	10.3
East Anglia	10.3	11.6	8.6	10.5
South West	11.3	12.8	9.2	11.7
West Midlands	15.1	17.7	11.4	14.8
East Midlands	12.4	14.5	9.5	12.3
Yorks & Humberside	14.6	17.2	10.8	14.4
North West	15.9	19.6	11.0	15.8
North	18.5	22.6	12.8	18.0
Wales	16.3	19.8	11.3	16.4
Scotland	15.3	18.8	10.8	15.0
Northern Ireland	20.9	26.4	13.6	20.9

Source: Department of Employment (1985) **Employment Gazette**, December, Table 2.3

Note: (a) Included in South East.

29

In Coventry, amongst the sample of home owner households interviewed who were economically active 7.8 per cent were seeking work at the time of the survey. Whereas these figures indicate that unemployment is not so prevalent amongst home owners as it is amongst tenants, unemployment rates do vary greatly within all sectors. In Coventry 16.7 per cent of householders living in areas at the bottom of the market – Hillfields and Charterhouse – were seeking work, compared with 5.0 per cent of those at the top – Allesley Park and Mount Nod. Any stereotype image of unemployment being principally a feature of local authority estates needs to be modified by a recognition that home owners may locally have also been members of high risk groups. Many who have entered home ownership in Coventry, particularly as first time buyers and working in manufacturing industry, have thus proved more susceptible, than the population of householders as a whole, to unemployment.

As high as these rates and levels of unemployment are they in some senses underestimate the incidence of unemployment. An important distinction is between the stock of the unemployed – those who are registered at a specified date – and the flow – those who become unemployed during a specified period. With 3 million people unemployed over the course of, say, a year many more will lose one job and get another. The Coventry survey can, again, be used to provide an example of the dynamics of unemployment. A comparison of household's employment status at the date of house purchase with that at the date of the survey shows that 18 per cent of the sampled households had experienced a net reduction in the number of their members who were employed, whilst 11 per cent experienced an increase. In the remaining 71 per cent of households the same number were employed. None of these figures should be taken to imply that it was the same people who were in work at the two dates, nor that some had not experienced several changes of employment status. It does indicate, however, both the fluidity of the relationship which households have with the labour market, and that against a background of general deterioration in employment levels some households have, in terms of raw numbers, been net winners. In fact, since purchase, 52 people in the 306 households sampled had ceased working mostly because of unemployment rather than retirement or death. Only 5 people had been re-employed and were working at the time of the survey. Set against this another 29 people who were not working when their households were bought were working when the survey was conducted.

Another illustration of the dynamics of unemployment is to be found in the number of people who had experienced unemployment, for however short a period, at least once since house purchase. Over the sample as a whole one fifth had been unemployed for an unspecified period of time. There was, however, considerable variation between housing areas with unemployment being particularly prevalent at the bottom half of the market (see Table 3.2).

The rates would be higher if expressed as percentages of those employed at time of purchase. Thus the figures indicate that in Coventry at least unemployment in home owner households has been widely experienced.

Table 3.2 Previous Experience of Unemployment since House Purchased by those Currently in Employment

Market sector	%
Top	8.2
Upper-Middle	10.9
Lower-Middle	49.5
Bottom	44.4
Total	22.7

Source: Coventry Household Survey.

A feature of unemployment in recent years is the increase in its duration. Throughout most of the post war period unemployment was generally a transitory experience consisting of two or three weeks between jobs. Long term unemployment was restricted to 'unemployable' people, that is those who for reasons of their physical or mental characteristics, including their behaviour and manner, made it difficult for them to find and hold on to employment. It remains the case that for many unemployment is a transitory experience, but the numbers of the long term unemployed have increased rapidly to incorporate both the 'unemployable' and the 'employable'. Thus, in 1971, 13.8 per cent of the unemployed in Great Britain had been unemployed for between 6 and 12 months, and a further 15.9 per cent for over 12 months. In 1980 when the total number of unemployed had about doubled the proportions of the long term unemployed had increased only slightly to 15.2 per cent and 19.0 per cent respectively. Figures provided by the Department of Employment do not extend more recently than 1980 for Great Britain, but do so for the UK as a whole. Since in 1980 the two areas had similar proportions of their unemployed who were long term employed this may not be a difficulty. The figures show a very rapid shift away from temporary unemployment. By 1985, 19.4 per cent had been unemployed for 6 to 12 months, and 41.0 per cent for over 12 months. Taking account of the increasing absolute numbers of unemployed these represent increases from 220,000 long term unemployed in 1981 to 1,950,000 in 1985. Over the same period very short term unemployment (that is a month or under) also increased from 210,000 to 380,000. Long term unemployment thus increased at five times the rate of short term unemployment.

Another of the features of unemployment in the 1980s has been its growth in the prime age group, that is the 25–44 age cohort. Even over the period from 1982–1985 the proportion of unemployment accounted for by this group rose from 33.7 per cent to 38.0 per cent. This rise was not due to an improvement in the relative position of younger or older people rather that unemployment has spread to groups who were traditonally more fortunate in the labour market. It does mean however that unemployment has increased amongst those who are conventionally the primary breadwinner group, at a period when the financial burdens of child rearing and home buying are particularly acute.

Welfare benefits

Another measure of the increasing incidence of poverty within the home ownership sector is the number of home owners who are in receipt of welfare benefits, particularly those which are means tested. Some benefits also have a specific element within them related to actual housing costs. This applies to both supplementary benefit (SB) claimed by mortgagors and housing benefit claimed by mortgagors and outright owners.

Supplementary benefit may be paid to householders who have no full-time employment. Other restrictions include those with savings in excess of £3,000 and those involved in trade disputes (though their families may be eligible). It does not cover such eventualities as the loss of overtime earnings and the loss of a first or a second income (unless both are lost). In 1967 there were 362,000 home owners in Great Britain who received SB. By 1976 this had increased to 410,000 and then in a cyclical fashion it increased to 721,000 in 1983 (DHSS 1986). Within that total the increase amongst those with mortgages, as opposed to outright owners, has been more rapid. The principal factor underlying these changes has been unemployment with the number of unemployed home owners with a mortgage receiving SB increasing five fold between 1978 and 1982 (DHSS 1983).

32

Although the system changed during 1987 at the time of our empirical research the basic amount of money received by those claiming SB was a sum related to the number of dependants and ages of those in the household, together with a sum equal to their actual mortgage interest, water rates and ground rent, and a nominal contribution towards property insurance and maintenance. Whereas certain elements of housing cost were paid in full, and this clearly helped to keep household in their homes, the system has limitations emanating from the low level of the payments. Thus in 1983 a single person on SB received only 23.3 per cent of the average net income of all single person households, whilst a married couple with one child received 39.3 per cent of the average for that household type (DHSS 1986). In addition, the amount received for property insurance and maintenance – £1.80 per week – was also low in relation to actual expenditure in these areas. A family consisting of two adults and two children and a £10,000 mortgage would receive in total less than £100 per week. Such financial circumstances may act as a modifying agent by protecting housing circumstances from the full force of unemployment. But they will not guarantee that changes to the consumption of housing (and other items) will not take place.

Since 1983 some home owners have been entitled to a rate rebate under the housing benefit system. Entitlement is means tested. Those on SB may get a full rebate, though this will not be so where, for example, there are non dependants (such as children over 18 who have left school or elderly relatives) living in the house. Those not on SB will receive some proportion of the full rates depending on their circumstances. In 1984 there were about 650,000 home owners receiving SB who got a rent rebate, and 1,600,000 not receiving SB who did so. Together they accounted for 17 per cent of all home owners in Great Britain. In Coventry, as a whole, the proportion was about 31 per cent indicating a much higher level of poverty.

As with the other phenomena considered in this Chapter there are large variations within the home owner sector with respects to such benefits. Table 3.3 shows the proportion of households in each of the Coventry study areas who received various state payments. Over half of the surveyed households received child benefit. This is not means tested and take up rates are generally close to 100 per cent so that the variation from area to area is directly related to the proportion of households with children. At the time of the survey child benefit was £6.85 per week so that it could represent a substantial addition to household incomes. Far fewer households received other benefits. Only 2.6 per cent received family income supplement and 7.9 per cent SB, both of which are means tested. Table 3.3 shows, however, that in each of the study areas there were some 'poor' families, but that they were particularly prevalent in the lower-middle and bottom ends of the market. They were also particularly drawn from first time buyers and mortgagors rather than subsequent buyers and outright owners.

Table 3.3 Households Receiving Social Welfare Payments and Pensions

	Family income supplement	Child benefit	Unemployment benefit	Supplementary benefit	Pensions
Mount Nod	-	57.8	-	-	8.9
Allesley Park	2.1	54.2	4.2	10.4	18.8
Cheylesmore	2.6	56.4	10.3	2.6	10.0
Poets Corner	-	52.1	4.2	6.3	2.1
Radford	5.4	62.2	13.5	5.4	5.4
Holbrooks	7.5	60.0	7.5	20.0	7.5
Charterhouse	-	37.5	16.7	12.5	8.3
Hillfields	4.5	36.4	4.5	9.1	13.6
Total	2.6	53.8	6.9	7.9	9.2

Source: Coventry Household Survey.

Mortgage interest subsidy

There now exists a fairly extensive literature on subsidies to home owners. Although there is no significant dissent from the view that home owners do receive subsidy there is not agreement about what this susbidy is or how it should be measured (see O'Sullivan 1984 for an excellent summary). In public, as opposed to academic debates, there is, however, general acceptance of the view that mortgage interest relief – a reduction on the rate of interest paid to the lender on the first £30,000 of the loan, which is proportional in size to the marginal rate of taxation of the borrower (known as MIRAS) – is the appropriate subsidy. It is this view which, for convenience, is also adopted here.

An issue, which has been extensively explored in relation to the MIRAS subsidy is that of equity. The government's own estimates carried out for the Housing Policy Review (DOE 1977) showed that tax relief rose steadily with income though not proportionately. The implication of their work was, then, that tax relief was progressive in effect. This has been disputed by Wilkinson and Wilkinson (1982), however. On the basis of further exploration of the data they argue that over the middle range of incomes, in which most home owners lie, the subsidy is roughly proportional to income. At the top end of incomes, however, the proportions increase so that it becomes regressive. More recent estimates (Johnson 1986) show that the £30,000 ceiling places an upper limit on the absolute amount of relief that a borrower can receive. As the ceiling has not kept pace with inflation the result has been that for increasing numbers of higher income earners relief has fallen as a percentage of income. It is clear from the evidence, therefore, that richer house buyers get more relief in absolute terms because they tend to have larger mortgages and higher marginal rates of taxation. To what extent the subsidy is progressive or regressive is, however, uncertain and, in any case, may change over time. Nevertheless, the various studies show that some groups of house buyers receive more subsidy than other groups. Because the studies all use highly aggregated data, however, the extent of intra group variation is unknown. For Coventry there is some evidence from our household survey.

The amount of mortgage interest relief received by each household was calculated on the basis of a number of assumptions: that buyers had not taken out a second mortgage or extended the first one; that they had annuity mortgages; and that they were not paying income tax at above the standard rate. Given the distribution of buyers' income this is not an unreasonable assumption.

In carrying out these calculations it is of course apparent that the 11.8 per cent of the sample who were outright buyers received no subsidy from MIRAS. Whilst this is a truism it highlights a feature of the housing finance system, namely, that it provides assistance with entry and not running costs. Over three quarters of the outright owners sampled had net household incomes under £100 per week and most were elderly or single parent households. Many of them would have faced costs of running their homes – maintenance, heating costs, rates and so on – which would be high in relation to their incomes. Although some of them may have benefitted from other subsidies, including improvement grants or housing benefit which are specifically housing subsidies, the major source of help to home owners – MIRAS – did not provide the outright owner with any assistance.

For those buyers in our sample with mortgages the median amount of subsidy they received was £547 per annum. This figure, however, conceals a wide variation. Table 3.4 shows that mortgagors at the top-end of the housing market, on average, received almost twice the subsidy of those at the bottom. This is not, however, a simple channelling of subsidy to buyers in high priced areas at the expense of buyers in low priced areas. Rather the subsidy received varied widely as between buyers in any one area. A number of buyers in Charterhouse and Hillfields received more subsidy than those in Mount Nod and Allesley Park, for example. The reason for this is that the amount of mortgage interest relief varies directly with the size of the mortgage and not with the price of the house itself.

This relationship means, in one sense, that MIRAS is well targetted where it is needed most. In other senses, however, it does not because, in general, households with larger mortgages have larger incomes. Their housing costs may be higher but, to an extent, that will reflect preference to consume over and above a basic amount of housing services. As with any other commodity purchased in the market place the amount which any household actually purchases will be a function, inter alia, of prices, preferences and incomes. Government may determine a minimum level of housing services but those who purchase more may be doing so out of preference rather than compulsion. The subsidy is proportional, not to housing need or low income, but to housing purchase expenditure or high income.

In considering the impact of mortgage interest relief on the demand for housing, however, there is an important distinction between formal subsidy and effective subsidy. Formal subsidy can be measured as the amount of interest relief which a borrower enjoys, whereas the effective subsidy is concerned with the extent to which all or part of this relief is capitalised, that is, causes a rise in house prices. Crucial, here, is the elasticity of supply of housing. If supply is totally inelastic then whatever the increase in demand there will be no corresponding increase in supply, so that the same stock of dwellings will be rationed out through higher prices. Existing owners of residential property will receive a windfall gain but buyers will face prices which have risen in line with the value of the subsidy. If the supply of housing is infinitely elastic, on the other hand, it will be fully responsive to the subsidy all of which is passed on to buyers.

Table 3.4 Amount of Subsidy by Area

(£ per annum)

Study area	Median	Subsidy Level: Minimum	Maximum	Number of cases
Mount Nod	716	199	1,192	36
Allesley Park	674	199	1,102	39
Cheylesmore	634	199	1,191	34
Poets Corner	578	79	854	32
Radford	516	60	735	33
Holbrooks	451	338	594	35
Charterhouse	387	119	497	17
Hillfields	378	199	528	17
Total	547	60	1,192	243

Source: Coventry Household Survey.

Unfortunately there are as yet no empirical studies which show the elasticity of supply in the U.K. O'Sullivan (1984) however has put forward an interesting proposition:

> 'A plausible ... hypothesis is that capitalization of existing formal subsidy has occurred to a greater extent on dwellings sought by low income households than higher income households. Thus the extent of tax capitalisation is a **negative** function of household income. The reason for expecting such differential tax capitalisation is the locational characteristics associated with housing. For low income households, access to fairly well defined local job markets is clearly important. Demand for dwellings in proximity to, say, a central business district is likely, then, to rise from lower income groups. Land for such dwellings – land being the input most likely to generate significant long run supply elasticities – is strictly limited. As one moves up the income scale the job market constraint becomes less binding and substitutability (between dwellings in different areas) more feasible. Hence supply becomes increasingly elastic. In the limit – for those at the top of the income scale – housing supply could well become infinitely elastic, suggesting a complete absence of capitalisation effects'. (p. 124).

This is clearly speculative but, if sustainable, has important implications for the diversity within home ownership. We have shown in the first part of this Chapter that there are, for a number of reasons, increasing numbers of lower income buyers. To an extent home ownership is coming to meet a major part of the housing needs of those with low incomes. The position of those with low incomes within the housing market, however, may be made worse by the present subsidy system. For the low income buyer who will tend to receive less MIRAS in any case, if this is entirely, or largely, capitalised then he or she will receive no assistance with housing costs from this source. In contrast the high income buyer receives more MIRAS and all, or most, contributes to a lowering of housing costs. It is possible then that the subsidy exacerbates rather than alleviates inequality in the owner occupier market.

The changing face of supply

The general question which this section seeks to address is how has the nature of the houses in which home owners live altered. As in the previous section this will not be answered by identifying the full range of possible developments. Rather the aim is to identify those aspects of the changes in supply which pose financial difficulties for home owners when set alongside changes in demand concomitant with increasing numbers of lower income home owners.

38

We have already noted that, in recent years, the home owner sector has increased, rapidly. To a large extent this has been achieved by changing the legal form of ownership; that is, transferring dwellings from public or private letting to home ownership. Most supply side changes occur relatively slowly, however. There are houses, still in existence and inhabited, which were constructed half a millenium or more ago. Very few houses survive that long: but in Britain survivors from the nineteenth century are not in the least rare. This is not simply a function of the durability and permanency of residential dwellings once they are built, but also of the high cost and the difficulty in providing additional housing quickly. At the national level, and even when the production of new build housing was high on the political agenda, such as during the 1950s, annual production never exceeded more than about 3 per cent of the total stock. At the local level the situation can be different with the housing stock being added to more quickly but in practice this has rarely meant rapid change. Generally, built-up areas have added to their housing stocks only slowly.

Not only may the absolute number of houses change slowly but also may the physical characteristics of the stock. Many of the towns which were developed as eighteenth century spa towns, as nineteenth century manufacturing centres or as twentieth century commuter settlements have retained a housing stock which physically reflects that origin. Generally, eighteenth century spa towns are characterized today by grand middle class terraces, nineteenth century manufacturing towns usually contain large numbers of working class, bye-law houses and twentieth century commuter settlements of low density semis.

The stock of jobs and of households will thus, generally, be less fixed than the stock of houses. Earlier in this Chapter it was shown how quickly and markedly levels of unemployment had changed, for example. In terms of the housing market and the distribution of the housing stock amongst individual households, this means that supply is more fixed than is demand. The frequent changes in the strength and nature of consumer demand are met by a housing stock which responds only slowly to those changes. In that sense the housing market is continually out of equilibrium. As the Housing Monitoring Team (1976) have argued:

> 'Stemming from the immobility and durability is [the fact] that any community will always be using a housing stock which is less than the current ideal. If it were possible to start all over again and instantly rebuild, communities would likely look quite different, although not necessarily better, but this is not possible. Hence society must constantly adapt the existing stock to serve current needs.' (p. 25)

This means that there is always likely to be a mismatch between supply and demand. What the population of an area want today will not be matched

39

fully by what the market can supply. What they will get will be some compromise based on modifications of the existing stock; modifications which are in the direction of, but not fully meeting, the present pattern of demand. Over time, then, there has been a series of ad hoc responses to changing patterns of demand, so that the housing stock has been modified continually as it has shifted towards changing 'equilibrium' states.

The ageing of the home owner stock

Another feature of the durability of the home owner stock is that in Britain, in recent years, its average age has increased. Changes in the average age of the stock have come about as a result of three main processes. The first is the transfer of housing into home ownership from another tenure. This has happened in Britain where throughout the course of the present century there has been a transfer of housing from the private rental sector. Of the 7.1 million private rental dwellings in England and Wales in 1914, 1.1 million were sold to home owners over the following 20 years. Likewise over the period 1939-1960, 1.5 million of the 6.6 million, which were in private renting in 1939, were similarly transferred. At the present time, the private rental sector which includes housing association stock has been reduced to about 2.2m. So that the transfer of pre-1919 World War One stock to home owners has largely been completed. There has been some limited transfer of pre-1919 stock into the local authority sector but the latter remains mainly dwellings built over the last 65 years.

The second and third processes are the demolition of existing stock and the addition of stock by construction. In a situation where over a one year period there was no demolition and no new building the average age of the housing stock would increase by one year. If there were no demolition but some new building or some demolition and no new building, or a share of each the average age could increase, decrease or remain the same. The crucial variables would be the numbers involved, and the average age of the demolished housing.

An indication of the extent to which these processes have resulted in an increase in the age of the home owner stock is given by Table 3.5. This shows that over the period 1969-1984 a larger proportion of mortgages were granted on pre-1919 dwellings with a smaller proportion on brand new dwellings. Although the decreasing proportion given on new dwellings is partly a reflection of the decline in new production, this does not seem to account entirely for the rising proportion of mortgages on pre-1919 dwellings. In particular, the latter has increased relative to all mortgages on second hand dwellings.

40

Table 3.5 Building Society Mortgage Advances by Date of Construction of Dwelling, U.K.

| | Advances on | | |
| | New dwellings | Pre–1919 dwellings | Pre–1919 dwellings as % non new dwellings |
	(000s)	(000s)	
1969	30.5	16.4	23.6
1974	24.9	18.7	24.9
1979	17.2	24.3	29.3
1984	12.1	27.1	30.8

Source: Housing and Construction Statistics.

Two more factors reinforce the significance of the statistical changes. Firstly, over the 15 years following 1969 some 2.5 million dwellings were added to the owner occupied stock as a result of new construction so that the stock of second hand dwellings has increased. Secondly, over the period 1980–1984 about 600,000 council houses, mainly built after 1919, have been sold to owner occupiers. The final column of Table 3.5 thus indicates that although the number of second hand houses built after 1919 has been increasing, the number of pre–1919 dwellings (or at least those on which a mortgage has been granted) has perhaps increased at a more rapid rate.

A similar picture is portrayed by a number of sample surveys although these are not strictly comparable; and each is subject to margins of error. The 1976 English House Condition Survey indicates that 28.1 per cent of owner occupied dwellings were built before 1919; the National Dwelling and Household Survey put the figure in 1977 at 30.9 per cent; and the 1981 English House Condition Survey at 32.6 per cent. At face value and given the annual increments to the stock through new build these proportions indicate a considerable transfer of houses from the private rental sector. It should be further noted that in 1981 29.2 per cent of the entire stock of 18.1 million dwellings in England had been built before 1919 so that on a pro rata basis the owner occupied sector contains more very old housing than does the stock as a whole.

What is the significance of this apparent ageing of the housing stock? It is not the case that older dwellings are necessarily of lower quality than new dwellings. Indeed some of the highest quality houses are the oldest. Nevertheless, a large proportion of surviving pre-1919 property is in the form of Victorian and Edwardian working class housing – built at high densities, poorly insulated, and with defective or non-existent damp proof courses. Moreover, there is evidence that, all other things being equal, the costs of maintenance and repair increase with the age of the dwelling. Stone (1970), for example, examined records on the costs of repairs and maintenance on a sample of local authority housing which, he argued, had been kept at a more or less constant level of repair. At 1964 prices he estimated the statistical relationship:

$$y = 5.0 + 0.4x$$

where y = the cost in £ of repairs and maintenance

x = age of the dwelling in years.

None of the dwellings in the sample had been built more than 40 years earlier but Stone felt confident in concluding that since 'the observations all lie so close to the time of fit ... it seems reasonable to assume the relationship with age would apply to dwellings much older than 40 years' (Stone 1970, p. 143). Whether or not this assumption is correct is an empirical question to which we do not have a conclusive response. The point is, however, that home owners are living in houses which are, on average, getting older. Not only are many of these houses – the large numbers of working class villas – often of lower quality than more modern houses, but there is a possibility that their repair costs per annum may also be rising. Broadly, therefore, it seems that as more of the pre-1919 housing is transferred to home ownership, and as the average age of the houses of home owners increases, their quality decreases and repair costs increase. So, on average, the homeowners stock is in worse condition now than it was in the past.

The costs of production

The real cost of producing, purchasing and maintaining housing has continued to increase in recent years, irrespective of tenure. Ball (1983) has identified a number of reasons why productivity in the construction industry has failed to increase as rapidly as in many other industries. One is that the production process which characterizes speculative housebuilding is not subject to the same intensity of pressure for technical change and productivity as is the case with most manufacturing industries. In most industries there is an incentive for all firms to follow the production methods of technically innovative ones. Being able to produce cheaper goods means that the latter can expand their shares of the market, and at the margin can exclude the non-technically innovative. In the case of the construction industry, the reduced profit from the process of construction can, however, be offset by profits which are made from the whole development process including land speculation. Thus 'an astute developer need not be an efficient organizer of production, and competition cannot force him to be except within very broad limits' (Ball 1983, p. 161).

Empirical evidence of the relative increase in cost over time is scanty because the various time series are confounded by changes in size and quality of the units constructed. However Morley (1977) presents an index which shows that:

> 'Between 1949 and 1975 – a period of 26 years – the cost of durable household goods increased by 170%, retail prices generally increased by 320% and housebuilding costs increased by 458% – a rate of increase no less than nearly three times that of durable household goods.' (Morley 1977, p. 9)

Morley further notes that the rate of increase in housebuilding costs has probably been faster for smaller, low-cost housing and thus the increase relative to average incomes has been greater for low income groups. The prices of both new and second hand houses have increased in line with the increases in cost. Table 6.1 shows that the increases have not been uniform with particularly large increases in 1972/3 and 1978/9. Nevertheless overall they have increased faster than prices generally, and continue to do so.

Finally, repairs and maintenance to housing, like its initial construction, have also become relatively more expensive. As activities they are essentially labour intensive with limited opportunities to adopt labour saving techniques, for example, by substituting capital. Processes such as external repainting or decorating have to be carried out in situ, often using techniques little different to those of 50 or more years ago. Although in some areas efficiencies have been achieved, as with factory-made replacement windows, the old ones still have to be taken out and the new ones put in, by hand. The construction of an index of relative costs is, for the same reasons as an index of housing construction costs, difficult.

A framework for consumer responses

The position at the present time, then, is the culmination of an extended period of national and widespread, individual prosperity. The expansion of home ownership to its present levels has been facilitated both by government housing policy and by a sustained post-war period of financial stability for a large proportion of the population. The degree to which housing needs are met for increasing numbers of households is directly linked to their ability to compete in the market place for owner occupied housing. In recent years, however, the widespread financial prosperity which underlay the growth of home ownership has been eroded. Unemployment and associated developments, have had an impact on some individual home owners, reducing their ability to compete. Indeed there is now a large group of home owners who have low incomes. Moreover, the durability of housing combined with its lack of replacement means home owners are living in homes which, on average, are getting older. Much was built prior to the onset of World War One and lacks many of the amenities or facilities which are usually found in more modern homes. Although housing is getting older and sometimes poorer in quality it is not getting cheaper. Those purchasing council homes have received large discounts on market prices, but most home owners face prices for both purchase and maintenance which have continued to increase faster than retail price inflation generally.

The concern here is not with why prices have kept rising even if the product is apparently inferior but with the consequences of the juxtaposition of low incomes and high prices. If reductions in demand by some consumers do not apparently manifest themselves in lower prices then how are they manifested?

Answers to such questions are not immediately obvious. Firstly, research and observation of the housing market has been largely confined to those situations in which prosperity and the ability to purchase housing were increasing. The studies of house price booms, the economic significance of home ownership, mobility and the family life cycle, filtering and housing ladders constitute a rich and diverse literature drawing on and emanating from a range of theoretical positions. But they are not rich and diverse in respect to the housing market contexts: these studies have been set within a framework of full employment, cheap mortgages and capital growth. The lessons from the literature of the 1960s and 1970s, therefore, may be of limited relevance to studies conducted during the 1980s.

Secondly, it might be anticipated that the consequences of the changed context could be deducted *a priori*. The usual reasoning would be that lower incomes would mean a shift in the market demand curve, leading to lower prices and lower consumption. In the case of the housing market the outcome may not be quite that simple. There are features of owner occupied housing as a commodity, and of its market which are different from many other commodities and markets. These differences influence the nature of the market outcome. In the remaining part of this Chapter we turn our attention to some of these differences. The objective is to set up a framework for understanding how

44

individual home owners respond to reductions in their ability to pay. In other words, it is to identify what there is about housing which structures the coping strategies of home owners who experience a fall in income, and what are the consequences of this for the market itself.

The distinctive characteristics of housing

Before discussing the range of coping strategies it is necessary to highlight three distinctive characteristics of housing.

A necessity. The point was made in Chapter one that housing is a necessity. By this is meant that if people are to lead 'normal' lives and to be considered part of 'normal' society, they require 'normal' housing circumstances. Of course this need not be owner occupied housing. Renting also meets the requirement. But for the person or family already in home ownership renting is frequently not a feasible or desirable option. Feasibility is, in part, defined by shortages. For local authority and housing association lettings, waiting lists are long. Many households – the young single, for example – have little realistic chance of access to such housing in most parts of the country. Many local authorities and housing associations, in any case, debar home owners except under certain circumstances. For its part the private rental sector in most areas of the country has decreased in size to such an extent that very few new lettings come on to the market. Desirability is restricted because of the perceived benefits of home ownership. The status of being a home owner and one of life's 'winners' as opposed to a tenant and one of life's 'losers' may be important. In so far as people have made financial sacrifices in order to better themselves, then moving to a rented dwelling will be seen as a retrograde step. The coping strategies of most home owners will thus be founded on a primary objective of retaining their home ownership status.

Complexity. In Chapter two it was argued that houses were physically complex. There is another sense in which houses are complex, however. In addition to the services such as location which may flow from a house, there is the investment potential of the house. In the case of rented housing the distinction is clear: the tenant receives the benefits of the flow of services whereas the landlord receives the benefit of the investment. For home owners both benefits are combined. Considerations of the amount and type of housing which an owner wishes to consume thus 'involves two highly-related decisions: (a) that concerning the amount of housing services he demands for consumption, and (b) that concerning the amount of capital stock he demands as an investment' (Struyk 1976, p. 28). This means, also, that the coping strategies of individual home owners will be structured by their objectives in relation to both aspects of home ownership.

45

Costs. Just as the benefits of housing are complex then so are its costs though not necessarily for the same reasons. Doling et al (1986) have argued that a distinction should be recognised between entry costs and running costs. Entry costs are those costs which face the individual entering the sector. These include transaction costs such as solicitors fees, stamp duty and land registration fees together with the capital cost of the legal interest in the dwelling. The capital cost or market value will, in practice, either be paid by a lump sum payment or, more commonly, with the help of a loan from a building society, bank, other financial institution or individual. In some cases the purchaser may obtain a loan, or loans, which cover the entire capital cost as well as furniture and legal fees. In other cases the purchaser will pay some proportion of the cost from savings including the equity on any house being sold. The widespread use of mortgages, there now being about 7 million households in Britain with mortgages on residential property, means that often the entry costs are spread over long periods of time, commonly 20 or 25 years.

Unlike entry costs, running costs are necessarily incurred throughout the entire period of ownership, and are necessary to maintain the flow of benefits from the home. In Britain today running costs include local authority rates though as a form of local tax there is no reason why they necessarily have to be tied to property ownership. In the longer term they may be raised in a different way which will disentangle them from running costs. Possibly the largest element of running costs is repairs and maintenance. Ingram and Oron (1977) suggest that the services provided by the physical structure are produced from the combination of: land, which is infinitely durable; operating inputs such as labour which are consumed during the process of production; and capital such as materials which have a range of durabilities.

'Housing is not a single durable commodity which is paid for at the outset and then gradually consumed over time. Rather, it consists of a set of capitals of varying durability. Thus the basic structure may be very durable, but the interior finish less durable. Over the course of the life of the house, and in order to maintain the quality of the services it provides, its various elements will require fresh inputs of capital. These inputs will occur irregularly and be met by lump sum payments from incomes or savings, or by loans.' (Doling et al 1986, p. 54)

The implications of this for a systematic maintenance programme have been considered by Gow (1985) who in a series of diagrams, one of which is reproduced here as Figure 3.2, shows the varying life spans of different building elements.

The range of coping strategies

Home owners derive a number of benefits from their tenure position and level of consumption of housing. In deciding to enter and remain in the sector,

46

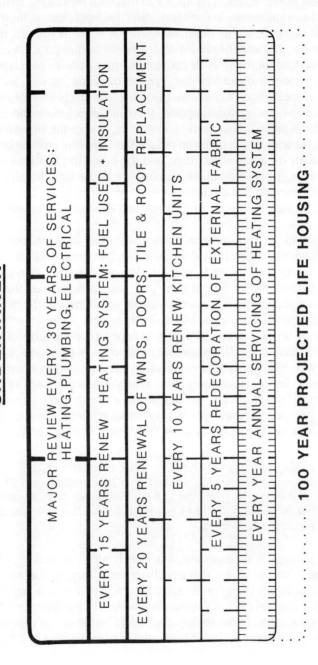

FULL MAINTENANCE MODERNISATION PROGRAMME

UNDERTAKEN

MAJOR REVIEW EVERY 30 YEARS OF SERVICES: HEATING, PLUMBING, ELECTRICAL

EVERY 15 YEARS RENEW HEATING SYSTEM: FUEL USED + INSULATION

EVERY 20 YEARS RENEWAL OF WNDS, DOORS, TILE & ROOF REPLACEMENT

EVERY 10 YEARS RENEW KITCHEN UNITS

EVERY 5 YEARS REDECORATION OF EXTERNAL FABRIC

EVERY YEAR ANNUAL SERVICING OF HEATING SYSTEM

100 YEAR PROJECTED LIFE HOUSING

Source: GOW (1985)

Figure 3.2 Maintenance Cycle

47

however, households incur a number of costs which over the market as a whole have increased in real terms. The ability to maintain these long term benefits and financial commitments, is for many, directly dependent on their position in the labour market. At this point we shall consider the options facing the home owner who has experienced a deterioration in that position and which in turn has reduced their ability to maintain former patterns of consumption. It is not our concern to examine the precise outcome for that will depend on a variety of individual circumstances such as the levels and nature of their housing and non-housing consumption, their incomes before and after their changed position in the labour market, and so on. Rather the aim is to examine the relative ease with which they can reduce their housing costs to bring them in line with their diminished incomes, and the broad implications of this for the level and type of reduction in the benefits they derive from housing. Implicit in this is an assumption that the behaviour of consumers in the housing market is influenced by their evaluation of the costs and benefits of alternative courses of action.

Considering, in the first instance, entry costs, these are faced only by those home owners with mortgages. By definition, outright owners will be concerned only with running costs which will be discussed below. For those with mortgages, reductions, both marginal and non-marginal, of their agreed monthly (occasionally weekly) loan repayments will often be difficult to achieve so long as they remain in the same house. There is some scope for retrenchment but this may be limited. One strategy is to renegotiate the term of the loan. The extent to which this will bring about a reduction in payments is, however, limited. In 1983, 57.2 per cent of outstanding building society loans had been taken out within the previous five years, which means that most of them had fifteen to twenty years to run. Yet extending a twenty year term to twenty five or to thirty years brings only a very small reduction in the amount of the monthly payment, as Doling et al (1986, p. 53) have shown:

> 'On an annuity mortgage of £10,000 at a rate of interest of 11.75 per cent the repayments over a 20 year term will be £109.90 per month, over a 25 year term £104.50, and over a 30 year term £101.60. The reduction in regular payment would thus be of the order of £1 per week for the first five year extension, and 75 pence for the second'.

A second strategy is to negotiate, with the lender, the making of interest only payments. For the lender this may have the advantage that although the size of the loan is not being reduced at least something is being paid back and the outstanding debt is not getting any larger. For the borrower it reduces the monthly repayment, by an amount dependent on the size of the outstanding loan and the rate of interest, and is particularly advantageous to SB claimants

48

receiving help with their mortgage interest repayments. In an earlier section the extent to which this was already happening was indicated. This possibility may not be open to everyone nor available in perpetuity, however. Some lenders may accept interest only payments for a limited period, say six months, before demanding repayments of capital. Others will not accept interest only payments at all, this apparently being the case for about 15 per cent of all local authorities (Doling et al 1986).

Where interest only payments are not accepted or where they do not represent a significantly large reduction, a third strategy may involve the size of the loan itself being substantially reduced. This may be achieved by a lump sum payment from savings (if they exist) though since mortgages have fiscally preferential treatment, whereas the savings may not, this is not necessarily a financially advantageous course of action.

If none of these options are open to the individual – if they already have a long repayment period, their lender will not accept (further) interest only payments, or if they have no substantial savings, for example – then the only way of reducing entry cost expenditure may be to sell the house and redeem the mortgage. In other words reductions in entry cost may be possible only by 'changing the product consumed rather than changing the repayment profile of the existing product' (Doling 1986, p. 53). This solution is far from unproblematic. Housing as we have pointed out in the previous section, is a necessity. If the household sells one house it will need to obtain another. Whether or not they can purchase another house will depend on the size of their equity holding in the house sold in relation to the prices of cheaper houses (if there are any) and how large a mortgage they can afford to repay (this may be zero). The equity may also be eroded by transaction costs involved in selling and buying, and as a result of any outstanding arrears in mortgage repayments. If owner occupied housing cannot be obtained it does not necessarily follow that rental housing can. The demise of the private landlord, and the inability and sometimes unwillingness of the public landlord to meet the housing needs of all ex home owners, may preclude this. For some therefore selling the family home may lead to moving in with parents or friends, and may lead to the breakup of the household.

If none of the strategies discussed above are possible, and those that are possible are not desirable, the mortgagor may seek other solutions. One is to reduce monthly mortgage payments by a unilateral decision not to pay them in full or even at all. In reality this may only be a short term solution since there will come a point where the mortgagee demands payment and then initiates a mortgage possession action through the county courts (see Doling et al 1985). In essence, therefore, there are similarities between the outcome of this and the selling up strategy.

Another solution, is not to reduce entry costs at all, but to continue to meet them in full and to make reductions in expenditure in other areas of the budget.

Such savings may be achieved not only on non housing expenditure but also on the running costs of housing, in particular in repairs and maintenance. The results of delaying periodic injections of investment necessary to replenish capital will generally be marginal in comparison with savings made in many non housing areas. Put crudely, if the household does not purchase food then its members go hungry, if it does not pay fuel bills they get cold, but if they do not repaint the exterior of the house it can be done next year or the year after next. To this extent repairs and maintenance like luxury items can be treated as a compensatory mechanism which can be used to regulate the effects of changes in income. It can also be considered as a form of dissaving or living off capital.

There are, however, clearly some items of repair and maintenance which will have an immediate impact. Broken central heating boilers, frozen pipes, broken windows and blocked drains are ignored not without immediate consequences. Moreover in the long run other areas of repairs and maintenance will have more marked consequences. In terms of the complexity of housing, discussed earlier, these consequences will be related to the physical structure rather than the neighbourhood or accessibility, and its flow of services rather than its investment.

Certain advantages of this outcome may be perceived. Cutting repairs and maintenance expenditure allows existing links with family, friends, social activities, and schools to be retained. Any adjustments to life style consequent upon unemployment or other causes of a fall in income are not compounded by the necessity for other large changes brought about by relocation. This strategy will also have a relatively minor affect on the investment potential of the house. Indeed we will argue later that there are strong market pressures, acting independently of income levels or unemployment, not to carry out repairs and maintenance.

The corollary of this is that if the owner wishes not to reduce consumption of these latter benefits this can only be achieved by selling the house and moving to another. The barriers to this, for those with reduced incomes, have been discussed above. In practice, therefore, the equity which people have in their homes may be difficult to unlock under circumstances of reduced income. Marcuse (1972) has described home ownership as a form of enforced savings and goes on to argue that it is a particularly illiquid form of saving. For those able to meet higher mortgage repayments equity can be released by obtaining an extension to a first mortgage, or another mortgage. It is evident that the extent of such 'leakage' is widespread (Kemeny and Thomas 1984). For those on low or falling incomes, however, the equity cannot be so readily unlocked.

In this section, therefore, we have sought to establish some of the constraints acting upon individual home owners whose financial position since the purchase of their home has deteriorated. Because of the nature of housing and the home ownership market, adjusting expenditure downwards is not unproblematic. The options open to different individuals will vary according to such factors as the amount of equity they have or their position in the housing market. The proposition is not, however, that these options and constraints are rigidly defined and cannot be transgressed: their behaviour is influenced in certain directions rather than determined. Collectively, home owners in this position will have a propensity to behave in certain ways so that regularities in their collective behaviour can be observed. It is these regularities in behaviour which form the foci of the following three Chapters.

Although we have concentrated on the cases of those individuals faced with an income loss, it is further posited that the same constraints and options have also influenced the behaviour of all those who are, by virtue of their income, marginal to home ownership. That is, that many of those with low incomes who have entered home ownership – unskilled and semi skilled manual workers, for example – may be faced with similar budgetary decisions and may perceive their options in similar ways. The following three Chapters therefore deal with empirical regularities in the behaviour of all low income home owners, irrespective of how they arrived at that position.

4 Mortgage Arrears

The costs of entry into home ownership are frequently met, at least in part, by the taking out of a loan. This is usually repaid on a monthly basis and over a period of twenty or twenty five years so that entry into the sector involves a regular and long term financial commitment. In practice this commitment is not always met, however. Individual borrowers may miss payments, in part or in full. The consequences of missed payment will depend on a number of factors such as the size of the monthly payment, the number of payments missed, the possibilities of repayment of the arrear and the willingness of the lender to enter into forbearance arrangements. In theory, however, the legal rights of the borrower are eroded by the missing of even one payment so that security of tenure comes into question at a very early stage. This is because the mortgage is a contract which has the effect of vesting the property in the lender as security for the loan granted to the borrower. Though, in practice, lenders may seek to obtain vacant possession in cases of default so that a loan can be recovered through selling the property unoccupied, in theory, and subject to any proviso in the deed, the lender has a right to possession – subject to Court approval – at any time (see Megarry and Wade 1984).

In the present Chapter we examine available evidence on the numbers of house buyers whose status as home owners has been threatened by their non payment of a mortgage. The Chapter goes on to identify the causes and consequences of this non payment. As in other Chapters the evidence is drawn together at national and local levels.

Trends in arrears

Unlike some other characteristics of housing markets, such as the number of loan advances made, a comprehensive picture of long term trends in mortgage arrears is not available. The longest running series is produced by the Chief Registrar of Friendly Societies. The relevance of this is limited, however, because it includes only those mortgages where the repayments are at least twelve months in arrear, or the property has been in the possession of the building society for at least twelve months. More recently the Building Societies Association has collated information, back to 1979, from the seventeen largest societies (which between them account for some 80 per cent of building society advances) about the number of properties taken into possession and the number of loans six to twelve months in arrear (Building Societies Association 1986). In 1984 Boleat (1984) published these same measures for the period 1969-1983 using information from an unspecified sample. Based on these Figure 4.1 shows a cyclical pattern with troughs in 1973 and 1979 and with peaks in 1970, 1976 and 1984. This broad pattern corresponds with that shown by the series, produced by the Registrar of Friendly Societies, of the number of loans over twelve months in arrears (see Doling et al 1985).

The increase since the 1979 trough has been particularly marked (Table 4.1). In 1979 there were 8,420 mortgages, 0.16 per cent of all building society mortgages, which were between six and twelve months in arrear. By 1985 this had increased sixfold to 49,630 being 0.74 per cent of all outstanding building society mortgages. This trend is substantiated further by figures published, for the first time in 1980, by the Lord Chancellor's Department and which provide information about actions in the county court for mortgage possession. In that year there were 27,105 actions taken by all types of lender including, in addition to the building societies, local authorities, banks, finance companies and individuals. Although the series was shortlived in its published form, the Lord Chancellor's Department has indicated that mortgage possession actions had grown to 64,301 by 1985.

The evidence provided from the survey carried out for the Association of Metropolitan Authorities (Culley and Downey 1986) suggests that for the period 1983-1985, at least, the pattern of increasing arrears has been common to both building societies and the local authorities in metropolitan areas. Thus in 1983 arrears were 0.7 per cent of total loan debt, with this proportion increasing by almost half to 1.0 per cent by 1985. Likewise, over the same period the proportion of loans at least 6 months in arrear rose from 2.7 per cent to 3.9 per cent.

Whereas the trends seem, on this limited evidence, to be broadly similar across lender types, the data are highly aggregated. The picture for individual building societies and individual local authorities can, in theory, be very different although, in practice, there is little published empirical evidence to show just how varied the pictures have been. Figures of arrears for Coventry

53

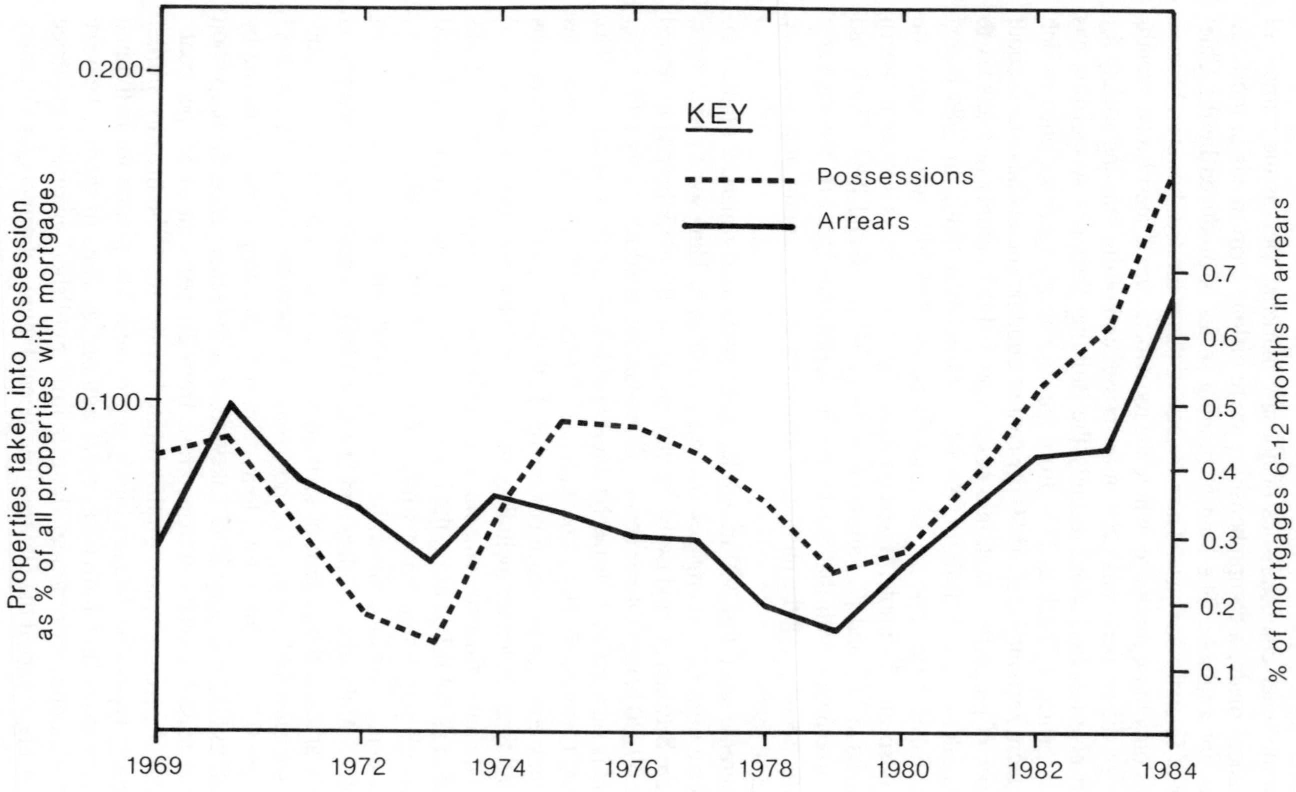

Figure 4.1 Default in Building Society Mortgages, 1969–1984

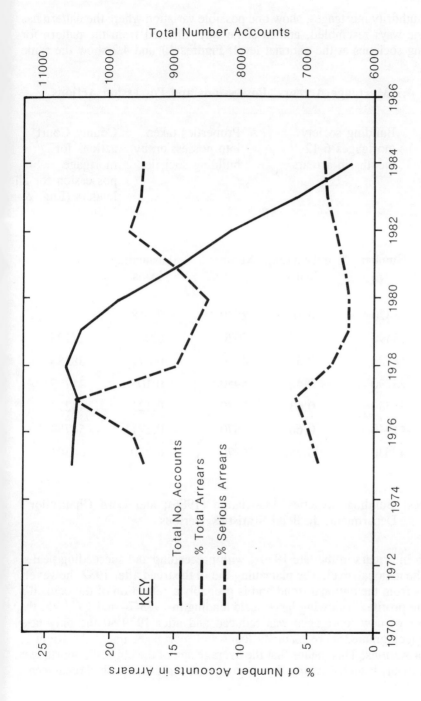

Figure 4.2 Default in Coventry Local Authority Mortgages 1975–1984

55

local authority mortgages, show one possible variation where the pattern has in some ways resembled, and in some ways differed from the pattern for building societies at the national level. Figures 4.1 and 4.2 show the same

Table 4.1 Mortgage Arrears, Possessions and Possession Actions

	Building society mortgages 6-12 months in arrears		Properties taken into possession by building societies		County Court actions for mortgage possession for all lenders (Eng. & Wales)
	Number	% outstanding loans	Number	% outstanding loans	
1979	8420	0.16	2530	0.048	-
1980	13490	0.25	3020	0.056	27105
1981	18720	0.34	4240	0.077	38284
1982	23790	0.42	5950	0.105	41799
1983	25580	0.43	7320	0.123	43274
1984	41940	0.66	10870	0.171	54754
1985	49630	0.74	16770	0.250	64301

Sources: Building Societies Association (1986); and Lord Chancellor's Department, **Judicial Statistics,** various.

trough in arrears in the late 1970s, with preceeding and succeeding peaks, as at the national level. The plateauing-out of the trend after 1982, however, differs from the national trend and is probably a reflection of the council's lending profile. Following large scale lending in 1973/74 and 1974/75, the number of new mortgages was reduced and after 1979/80 the only new mortgages granted were maturity loans and mortgages under the Right to Buy provisions. This means that the average age of the council's mortgages has probably been increasing. Since arrears are more likely when repayments are a large proportion of income (Ford 1986), that is often when they are young, it is to be expected that the increasing average age of the outstanding mortgage portfolio would deflate arrear levels. Even so by 1984 one in six council borrowers was in arrear at any one time, and one in twenty-eight was at least three months in arrear. Nevertheless the example of Coventry does illustrate the fact that it cannot be assumed that trends at the national level are necessarily repeated at all local levels or for all lenders.

Levels of arrears

Although the available statistical information is consistent in its portrayal of the direction of change, there are doubts about the actual level of the failure of mortgagors to meet the financial commitment of home ownership. These doubts centre on the appropriateness of the period at which arrears are included in the statistics. Thus the BSA does not record arrears of less than six months. By implication this might be taken to suggest that arrears of one to five months are of no concern. This issue has been addressed by Ford and Took (1986) who argue:

> 'The decision to present arrears statistics in terms of those owing six or more months payments is an arbitrary one. The recent BSA publication on arrears provides no rationale for such a decision, simply asserting "it is appropriate to focus on figures for loans 6-12 months in arrears" ... The outcome of such decisions is that the institutional statistics (that in the absence of other sources are treated as if they were the official statistics) provide no information on the number of borrowers that have arrears of less than six months payments, and as such offer a persistently incomplete account that feeds into the public arena a particular view of the issue,' (p. 9)

The significance of the apparently arbitrary choice of six months as the point at which to start recording arrears has received further legitimation, however, by the decision of others to present their statistics according to the same criterion for purposes of comparison. The Department of the Environment (1985) for example, notes that the decision to change their earlier practice of relying on local authorities' own accounting systems, which generally included arrears of one month or more, as the appropriate measure of arrears was 'made to bring local authority figures into line with building society statistics' (p. 2). Culley and Downey (1985) have also organised data to make this same comparison, adding the label 'serious' to describe such arrears and to distinguish them from 'medium level' (3-6 months) and 'casual' (1-3 months).

So what is being established by these decisions is a view that what is important in public policy and management terms is how many accounts are at least six months in arrear. The implicit dismissal of shorter arrear periods is not, however, unproblematic. Many lending institutions take arrears at points below six months as the trigger for instituting legal proceedings. Of the borrowers facing mortgage possession actions in 1982 in Coventry County Court, for example, 33.1 per cent were under 6 months, and 19.4 per cent under four months in arrears (Doling et al 1984). Any popular perceptions, derived from published statistics, of the extent to which mortgagors are failing to meet their payments are thus based on statistical information which arguably underestimates the actual extent of the threat to security of tenure.

Ford and Took (1986) have also attempted to estimate what this actual extent might be. They took as their starting point the proposition that many of those accounts which were just one month in arrears would have been 'technical' arrears. For example, a standing order had not been amended following notification from a society of an increase in repayments, or it was delayed in transmission. These were arrears, then, which in a sense were accidental and would be quickly rectified. They further argued that most arrears of two or more months were not technical arrears. The twenty building societies who provided them with data on accounts owing two or more months payments accounted for about 70 per cent of all the mortgages advanced by building societies. The information showed that, on average, 2.2 per cent of all mortgages were two months in arrears, with a further 2.4 per cent three or more months in arrears. The authors concluded that since there were, in 1985, 6 million or so outstanding mortgages, almost 300,000 of them would have been two or more months in arrears.

Since Ford and Took concentrate exclusively on building society mortgages, even these figures, would probably underestimate the scale of mortgage arrears, however. In 1985 building societies were responsible for 83 per cent of the loan advances made by institutions, with the banks being responsible for 14 per cent, the insurance companies 1 per cent and local authorities 2 per cent. In addition, unknown numbers of mortgages are advanced by finance companies and private individuals. Very little is publicly known about the arrear profiles of these various organizations though there is some evidence that the banks tend to have low levels and the finance companies high levels of arrears (Doling et al 1985). There is, moreover, some systematic evidence of the position of local authorities and this points to their generally higher levels of arrears. Thus Table 4.2 indicates that the rates for those five to twelve months in arrear in comparison with building societies were four times higher amongst local authorities, and for possessions one and a half times higher. Although it has been argued that the two samples are not necessarily representative – the 30 local authorities include 23 London boroughs, for example – the generally higher rates amongst local authorities has been confirmed by more recent research. The DOE figures, for example, indicate that 2.3 per cent of all outstanding local authority loans are six to twelve months in arrears, this being about three times the building societies figure of 0.74 per cent (Department of Environment 1985). On the basis of these indications, then, Ford and Took's estimate might be increased to perhaps 350,000 people being at least two months in arrears.

Table 4.2 Building Society and Local Authority Mortgage Arrears 1976

	No. mortgages outstanding	5-12 Months arrears		Possession actions	
		No.	%	No.	%
4 Building Societies	1,494,000	5,259	0.35	1,224	0.082
30 Local Authorities	170,000	2,360	1.39	221	0.13

Source: Finnis, N. (1978).

If this estimate is much larger than usually supposed, the scale of mortgage default is actually possibly even larger. The underestimate arises because it is based on cross sectional data, measuring the number of borrowers in arrears at a particular point in time. A longitudinal study, however, would doubtless reveal that over the previous year (or any other period) some buyers had both fallen into arrears and then cleared them. In other words, the proportion of house buyers whose security of tenure has been at risk – due to being in arrears – will be higher than the 5 or 6 per cent suggested by cross sectional studies.

The significance of this argument can be gauged by the results of the Coventry household survey. Of the 269 respondents with mortgages only 7 (2.6 per cent) were in arrear at the time of the survey. However, since buying their home – a period of up to five years – 25 (9.3 per cent) of the sample had been in arrears at least once. Further an additional 27 (10.0 per cent) said that since they had bought they had experienced at least one occasion when they thought they might be unable to meet their mortgage repayments. Although the survey areas were selected from different sectors of the market, the sample was not representative of all buyers and the results cannot be simply generalised. Nevertheless there is a strong indication that. arrears are not infrequent incidents. Far from being a minor aberration the failure to meet the long term financial commitments of home ownership is actually widespread.

This point can be reinforced if we consider mortgage arrears in monetary terms. Bearing in mind that most outstanding mortgages have only recently been initiated we can assume that the average amount owed by those two or more months in arrears is, say, £350. This would, in fact, represent, at current rates of interest, something like a three month arrear on a loan of £12,000 so that, arguably, it is a conservative estimate. Since there are perhaps around 300,000 borrowers two or more months in arrears, the total sum involved is of the order of £100 million. This sum can be put into perspective by reference to the total sum of public sector rent arrears, which has been given as £150 million (Hansard 19 February 1986). This figure includes arrears of less than two months and also amounts owed by sources other than tenants, specifically the Department of Health and Social Security. It would seem on the basis of these figures alone, therefore, that it would be difficult to determine whether total mortgage arrears were larger or smaller than rent arrears. Given that it is commonly recognized that local authorities house many of the poorer sectors of society – the broad equality in debt indicates the dimension and the significance of arrears amongst home owners.

Where, what and whom

There is comparatively little evidence about how the incidence of arrears can be broken down; whether, in relation to the number of borrowers, there are more arrears in some parts of the country than others, in some parts of the housing market, amongst certain types of household and so on. This information is important in its own right but also because it can provide an empirical basis for the identification of the causes of arrears. If it is discovered that arrears are, pro rata, higher amongst the unemployed or the young, for example, these are facts which may help both the formation and the testing of hypotheses about the processes which give rise to arrears. They also help to illuminate the nature of the constraints and options facing home owners in different circumstances. Until recently this empirical information has been largely anecdotal in origin. Some systematic evidence has been produced recently, however, which suggests a number of empirical regularities. These are presented here.

Regional variations

The lack of evidence on regional variations in arrears and possessions is typical of the patchy coverage of published information. To the authors' knowledge there are no published data which give a regional breakdown of arrears other for local authority mortgages. These data, which have been collected by the DOE, are summarized in Table 4.3. Alongside these are the results of a study of the 1,026 repossessions carried out by the Halifax Building Society between February 1984 and January 1985 which have been compared with the regional distribution of loans over the same period (Southwell 1985). Because lending patterns do not remain constant, the regional possession rates shown in Table 4.3 are approximate. The pictures which emerge from these two sources are roughly similar. Arrears and possessions are lower south of a line from the Wash to the Bristol Channel, though Scotland (and possibly Northern Ireland) are exceptions. There are important differences also, however. Local authority arrears, in relation to Halifax Building Society possessions, are high in Greater London and low in the West Midlands for example. Unfortunately, it is not possible to decide whether the regional pattern of arrears and possessions actually do differ in the way described, or they are the same but sampling characteristics have produced the differences. Essentially this is a problem of the extent to which either set of information can be generalized. The local authorities account for only around 10 per cent of outstanding mortgages and these will, in any case, tend to be towards the lower end of the market; the Halifax Building Society is the largest in Britain but its lending is not necessarily typical of all building societies or of all lenders.

Roughly the same picture is, however, also apparent from data about the number of possession actions sought by all types of lender. This information is compiled by the Lord Chancellor's Department from the returns made by each county court in England and Wales. Its strength is that because it records actions by all borrowers it 'can tell us something about the scale of default experienced in an area as a whole rather than the experience of one lender whose lending profile and arrears management may or may not be typical' (Doling and Stafford 1987). Its limitation is that the areas over which county courts have jurisdiction do not coincide precisely with local authority or other areas used for statistical purposes. Consequently the comparison of mortgage possession actions with other variables such as the number of house buyers or unemployment is not easy. In terms of a broad regional picture, however, this can be overcome by aggregating the data to the level of county court Circuits, as shown in Figure 4.3. Table 4.4 then provides statistical information for the Circuits which show a pattern similar to that of Table 4.3; a north-south divide with posession action rates of 32 per 1,000 in London and 49 per 1,000 in the rest of the South East, rising to 102 per 1,000 in the Midland and Oxford Circuit.

Market position

If the evidence of variation in the incidence of arrears by region is scanty then that is even more so of their incidence by market position. On a national level we simply do not know whether arrears are mainly associated with

Table 4.3 Regional Variations in Arrears and Possessions

Region	Local authority arrears[a] 1983/84		Halifax Building Society[b] possessions 1984/5
	Number of outstanding loans	% of loans 6 or months in arrears	% of loans possessed
Northern	33,300	2.6	0.38
Yorks & Humberside	58,600	2.5	0.45
East Midlands	49,100	1.9	) 0.34
Eastern	58,400	1.6	)
Greater London	129,500	2.4	0.24
South East	83,200	1.9	0.10
South West	50,900	1.7	0.23
West Midlands	73,200	2.0	0.59
North West	99,600	3.4	0.92
England	635,600	2.3	-
Wales	-	-	0.73
Scotland	-	-	0.27
Nothern Ireland	-	-	0.12[c]

Notes:

(a) Department of the Environment (1985)

(b) Southwell (1985)

(c) The number of cases is small and the findings should be treated with caution.

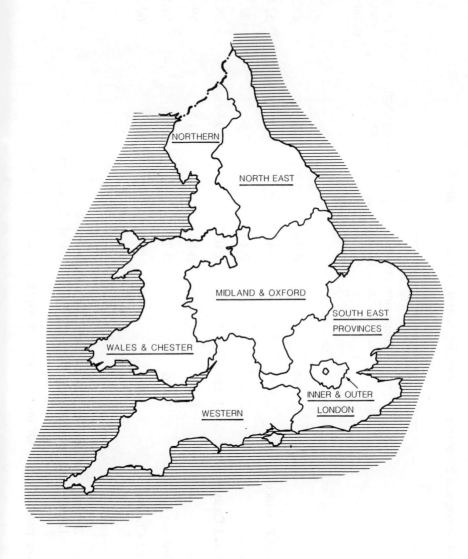

NORTHERN

NORTH EAST

MIDLAND & OXFORD

SOUTH EAST
PROVINCES

WALES & CHESTER

INNER & OUTER
LONDON

WESTERN

Figure 4.3 Country Court Circuits in England and Wales

Table 4.4 Mortgage Possession Actions by County Court Circuits 1982

Circuit	Possession actions		Unemployment rate	Per cent owner occupiers
	Number	% of mortgagors		
London	2,598	0.36	9.3	48.5
South East Provinces	8,959	0.49	6.9	62.0
Western	3,900	0.64	7.9	62.7
Midland and Oxford	11,556	1.02	10.9	58.5
Northern	6,641	0.96	13.1	59.1
North East	5,476	0.72	12.8	51.9
Wales and Chester	3,209	(a)	12.4	60.7

Sources: Statistics provided by Lord Chancellor's Department; Department of the Environment (1979); Census of Population, 1981.

(a) No comparable figure for the number of mortgagors has been found.

cheaper or more expensive homes, with starter homes, ex–council houses or the traditional stock, or with inner city or suburban housing. At the local level the evidence of the actions for possession entered in Coventry County Court in 1981 and 1982 does allow some conclusions to be drawn for that city about the properties involved. It shows that they have occurred right across the housing stock.

Table 4.5 shows the rateable values of the properties involved in cases in 1982. Nationally there is a strong correlation ($r^2 = 0.99$) between the square of rateable value and capital value (Robinson 1981), so rateable values might be taken to give a broad picture of the variation in house prices. Since the average domestic rateable value in Coventry in 1982 was £193.85 (CIPFA 1982) it follows that the properties involved were from all sectors of the owner occupied market. This is confirmed by the geographical distribution of the properties which have been mapped in Figure 4.4. With the exception of the south west corner, which is for Coventry one of the most expensive areas, and the north west, which is largely undeveloped, the properties are fairly randomly distributed. On the basis of this evidence, then, it would be difficult to come to the conclusion that possession actions were confined to inner city properties, or to properties in any particular sector of the Coventry housing market.

This does not mean, however, that there is no systematic bias in the occurrence of mortgage arrears with respect to market position. The Coventry household survey provides evidence that although arrears occur throughout the market they are more likely to occur at the lower than at the upper end. Table 4.6 shows that in one area – Holbrooks – 30 per cent of buyers interviewed had been in arrears at least once since buying their home. Unfortunately it is unknown whether this same finding would be applicable to other parts of the country or whether it is something peculiar to Coventry.

The buyers

Again, the evidence about the characteristics of those in arrears, in comparison with those borrowers who were not, is both disparate and sketchy. The most comprehensive piece of work in this area has been carried out by Ford (1984) who has summarized her results thus:

> 'While there is considerable spread on many of the variables (age, income, amount owed, type of property involved) the arrears profile is more heavily weighted towards young borrowers who are or have been clerical and semi-skilled workers, and also first time buyers often with higher than average percentage loans.' (p. 11)

In this section we look at some of these characteristics, individually, placing particular emphasis on the findings of the Coventry household survey.

65

Table 4.5 Rateable Value by Plaintiff Type, 1982

	Local authority	Finance/ property co.	Building society	Total
Under £100	11.4	–	2.4	4.5
£100 – 149	20.0	30.8	16.2	18.5
£150 – 199	33.4	33.3	33.6	33.2
£200 – 249	23.8	30.8	31.9	29.3
£250 – 299	10.4	5.1	10.1	10.0
£300 – 349	–	–	3.4	2.5
Over £350	1.0	–	2.4	2.0
Mean	178	176	202	194
Number of Cases	105	39	295	447

Source: Doling, J., Karn, V. and Stafford, B. (1984).

Age Although in five of the seven areas in Coventry in which households had been in arrears their median ages were lower than the median ages of non arrear households the relationship is not strong (Table 4.6). This contrasts markedly with Ford's results and also with Southwell's (Southwell 1985) where on a pro rata basis there were almost twice as many homes were possessed where the head of household was under 25.

First time buyers Table 4.6 shows that in Coventry seventeen of the twenty-four households in arrears, for whom there was knowledge of whether they were first time buyers or not, were in fact first time buyers. This supports Ford's finding in relation to Abbey National Building Society arrears that:

> 'two thirds of those in arrears are first time buyers, the largest group of whom had previously been living with relatives.' (Ford 1984, p. 7)

Occupational type In the Coventry sample, households in arrears were drawn mainly from those in skilled and semi-skilled occupations this being so both in absolute terms and in relation to the total number of households in these occupations. This differs from Ford's findings which showed, pro rata, a higher incidence of arrears amongst junior non-manual and unskilled manual, but not amongst skilled manual.

Key
• Building Society
○ Local Authority
+ Other Lender

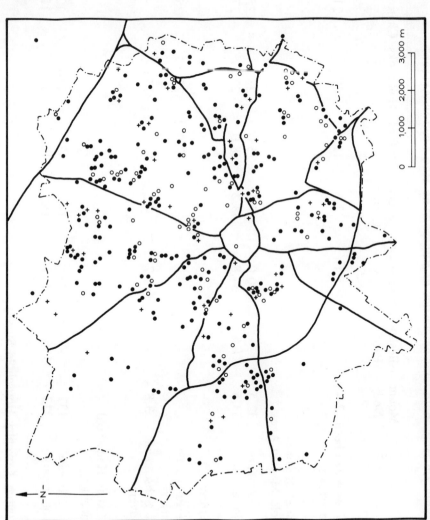

Figure 4.4 Mortgage Possession Actions in Coventry

Table 4.6 Household Characteristics of Buyers Who Had Been in Arrears

	Mount Nod	Allesley Park	Cheylesmore	Poets Corner	Radford	Holbrooks	Charterhouse	Hillfields	Total
% who had been in arrears	2.4	-	5.1	2.6	11.8	30.6	21.1	10.5	9.3
Head of Household Median Age:									
Arrears	32.5	-	30.0	37.5	25.0	28.3	25.0	30.0	28.7
Not arrears	33.5	31.5	34.8	33.2	28.0	27.2	27.5	31.7	31.0
Arrears:									
% First time buyers	-	-	-	-	12.0	25.0	25.0	13.3	11.0
% Subsequent buyers	3.8	-	4.2	4.2	12.5	75.0	-	-	6.3
Median Household Income:									
Arrears	137	-	331	112	137	110	121	72	125
Not arrears	212	186	196	185	138	113	121	133	167

Source: Coventry Household Survey

Incomes Table 4.6 shows the median weekly household incomes of arrears' and non arrears' households in Coventry. Generally, those who had been in arrear had lower median incomes, the exceptions being Charterhouse where the median equalled that of the non arrears' households, and in Cheylesmore where the one household in arrear had an unusually high income. The preponderance of lower income households amongst arrears cases was also apparent in the Ford study.

Causes of arrears

The processes which have lead to these empirical patterns over time and space are as little researched as the patterns themselves. Although there is a growing body of research into the causes and other aspects of mortgage arrears the results provide only a number of partial pictures which can at best be moulded together and along with a certain amount of speculation lead to the most tentative of generalisations. What emerges is a series of more or less reasonable explanations of circumstances in which some people fall behind with their mortgage payments. In the course of this much is revealed about the relative instability of the tenure position of home owners and about the speculations made in Chapter three about constraints and options facing home owners.

We can begin by reference to a classification produced by Merrett (1982) in which he places the causes of arrears under two headings. The first is when the household's income remains broadly constant, but where an arrear may arise for a number of reasons. The household budget may be mismanaged, the household borrows too much, or there may be unavoidable increases in expenditure such as when the interest rate rises. The second situation is where there is an unanticipated fall in household income. This may be because of either employment changes resulting from redundancy, dismissal, pregnancy or illness, or the break up of the household.

Although Merrett was correct in claiming that 'no quantitative estimates have yet been made of the relative significance of these factors' (p. 114), more recently there have been attempts to untangle the affect of these various circumstances on mortgage arrears as well as the broad balance between them. The Building Societies Association's report (BSA 1985), for example, concluded:

> 'Matrimonial problems are the single most important cause of arrears. The more serious the arrears the more likely there are to be matrimonial problems. Matrimonial problems occur in 30-40% of all possession cases.

> 'Financial mismanagement seems to be responsible for about 20% of arrears problems, and unemployment for about 40%.

69

'Over time the extension of building society lending criteria and competition in the mortgage market may increase the levels of arrears and possessions. Also the easier availability of second mortgages and credit generally may be making it more difficult for some people to maintain the basic mortgage repayments.' (BSA 1985, p. 39)

The foundation for these estimates, other than casual observation by the members of the BSA working party, is unclear. Indeed the one piece of systematic empirical research cited by the report came to a somewhat different conclusion about the relative importance of the causes:

'The reported causes of arrears are multiple. The data suggest that unemployment is an important influence upon arrears, although accounting for under 50% of arrears. As significant is the excessive level of financial commitment that borrowers take on. Matrimonial dispute, although widely believed to be an important component in the development of arrears, is in practice not implicated except in a handful of cases.' (Ford 1984, p. 28)

Southwell's investigation of the causes of arrears, which drew upon the branch manager's assessment of each case of possession provides yet another picture. The most common causes attributed were 'wilful' (45 per cent), 'failure to cope' (20 per cent), 'marital problems' (19 per cent) and 'unemployment' (12 per cent). This finding is clearly at odds with both the BSA and the Ford findings. This may be because of real differences in the experiences of borrowers with the one building society on which Southwell was reporting. Alternatively it may be saying something about the nature of the building society itself, in particular the perceptions of its managers. Indeed Southwell warns:

'The frequent use of the four main categories suggests that there is guidance on classification from Head Office, and it may be that branch staff ascribe cases to one or other cause without giving the matter a great deal of consideration. The categories themselves are not as specific as they might be, so that it is necessary to bear in mind possible limitations in the data.' (p. 25)

Perhaps significantly, quite a different picture is acquired from asking borrowers, rather than lenders, the reasons for their falling behind with payments. Of the 22 households in the Coventry sample who gave a reason, 10 said that unemployment was the critical factor, with a further 2 identifying other 'recession' factors, namely short time working and lack of overtime. In contrast, only 1 put their difficulties down to 'marital breakdown', with 3 citing 'illness' and 3 'lack of money'.

At the present stage of empirical research, therefore, there is a great degree of inconclusiveness about the relative importance of different events and circumstances in leading to arrears. One thing which complicates the analysis is that, in practice, individual cases of borrowers in arrears do not always fall into any neat typology. Their circumstances are generally complex in a number of ways. Arrears may be the result of more than one precipitating factor. Unemployment and its financial and psychological consequences may lead to marital break up. A given level of ability, or inability, to budget might be sufficient to cope at one level of income or level of commitment but not at others. The loss of a second income through pregnancy might coincide with an increase in the mortgage rate and a major repair bill. It is also important to appreciate that any inconclusiveness in the identification of causes may not arise because of any methodological or conceptual limitations, but simply because the samples examined to date have actually differed. What causes arrears which result in possessions may be different to what causes arrears in general; what were significant causes in 1980 may not be so significant in 1985; and what causes arrears in the south east may be different to what causes them in the north east. It cannot, in other words, necessarily be assumed that the processes are everywhere and at everytime equally existent or potent.

Given this complexity an alternative approach is to examine the theoretical implications of certain events and factors, such as marital breakdown and unemployment, on the ability and willingness of the household to continue to meet mortgage repayments. This involves looking at trends in presumed relevant events and factors and relating those trends to what is known about trends in mortgage arrears. Methodologically this also has limitations, not least because it involves inferring from what has been happening generally to what has happened specifically. Nevertheless the analysis substantiates the importance of a number of factors in explaining the incidence of mortgage arrears.

The social pathology explanation

We have already referred to Southwell's findings that the assessment of the branch managers of one building society was that 45 per cent of possession cases had arisen because borrowers were 'wilful' and a further 20 per cent because of a 'failure to cope'. These findings are indicative of a frequent assertion that mortgage arrears result when borrowers fail to manage their financial affairs. In essence the borrower, as an individual, is blamed for his or her debt(s). This is a social pathological explanation of mortgage arrears. The defaulter is seen as 'feckless', someone who 'won't pay' rather than 'can't pay'. The arrear represents a 'wilful' refusal by the mortgagor to meet his or her legal obligations. A more sophisticated version of the social pathology explanation would stress that defaulters lack the initiative, education and social skills (especially budgetting) to remedy their situation. In short, their value system and life style engender mortgage default. These 'accusations' are in fact reminiscent of comments made about tenants with rent arrears as Duncan and Kirby (1983) attest:

'It is often suggested by housing management staff that tenants who get into arrears organise their money badly' (p. 50) and,

'It is sometimes suggested that tenants in arrears live beyond their means and that debt is a result of over-indulgence in luxury items or a deliberate use of the housing department as a source of interest free credit.' (p. 51)

The Coventry survey provides some evidence of the general falsity of such assertions in relation to mortgage arrears. The first step in this evidence involves looking at the ways in which households manage their financial affairs (see Pahl 1980, 1983, 1984, 1985; Land 1983; and Ashley 1983). Some of these ways appear to be 'rational' and to provide the basis for sound budgetting. This applies, for example, to the 'independent management system' whereby each partner has an income and is responsible for specific items of expenditure. Other ways may appear to be less rational. The 'crisis' system, whereby households attempt to cope with each bill as it occurs and in a piecemeal fashion, falls into this category. The extent to which these different systems are rational or not, is debatable, and there is of course a difference between planning and execution. The results of the Coventry survey, however, show that for the different financial management systems there were no significant differences between the proportions of those who had, and those who had not, been in arrears.

Equally there were few differences in the range of financial commitments by those in and those not in arrears. The proportion of households in each of the Coventry survey areas which had outstanding hire purchase/credit sale was about a quarter, mail order payments about a third and TV rental about a third. In addition to there being relatively little variation in these expenditures between areas there were also no significant variations between those who had been in arrears and those who had not. The same applied to the ownership of credit cards. Indeed the only significant difference found (at the 0.05 level) was that having been in arrears was associated with *not* having a telephone.

There was, therefore, no empirical foundation in the Coventry survey findings for a social pathology explanation for mortgage arrears. More generally, however, this explanation can be criticized as being simplistic and mechanistic. It ignores the fact that social action is influenced by the subjective meaning individuals assign to a situation and that external events, like economic change, enable (or constrain) behaviour. Further at the empirical level it cannot explain the recent rapid increase in arrears since 1979 as there is no evidence that borrowers have become more 'wilful' or inadequate since then. It is useful to provide support for this critical position by referring again to Duncan and Kirby (1983):

'The survey evidence suggests that, at worst, extravagance is a factor in only a minority of cases ... In general, responses indicated that tenants in serious arrears were not unlike those in the random sample of all council tenants in their approach to budgeting and financial management.' (p. 51)

Marital breakdown

Marital and relationship breakdown have increased in recent years. In 1970 there were four decrees absolute granted per thousand married couples in England and Wales. Ten years later the rate had tripled to twelve per thousand. It is not difficult to appreciate how some mortgage arrears arise as a consequence of the breakdown in the relationship between two people – with or without children – who are buying a house. Two households are formed where one existed previously and their combined living costs (buying two houses instead of one or buying one and renting another) may be increased. If one partner stays in the family home then there may be financial difficulties in meeting the mortgage repayments. The payment of the mortgage may itself be the subject of dispute with neither partner being willing to maintain the repayments. There may also be difficulties arising from the failure of the social security system to act according to its own rules (see Tunnard 1976). Empirically the main limitation of the marital breakdown explanation is that whereas arrears rates have increased rapidly since 1979, marital breakdown rates have increased only slowly (Doling et al 1985).

Unemployment

In Chapter three we saw that unemployment in Britain has increased several fold in recent years and over the period since 1970 has shown the same cyclical pattern as mortgage arrears. It is a conformity in their W shapes which indicates a correlation between them. Supporting statistical evidence is also contained in Table 4.4 which shows broadly, that those areas in the south of the country with the lowest possession action rates also have the lowest unemployment rates. This relationship is also apparent at the local level. From the addresses given in the files held by Coventry Council Court it is possible to locate the electoral ward of each property, and then using information from the Census to calculate the number of possession actions in 1981 and 1982 per 1,000 home owners. Since the number of mortgagors, as opposed to outright owners, is unknown this rate is an underestimate of the 'risk' facing mortgagors. The 1981 Census also provides information, at ward level of numbers seeking work. As a rate of unemployment this can be graphed, as in Figure 4.5, with the possession rate. Giving a rank correlation of $r = 0.75$ this indicates a significant relationship between possession actions and unemployment rates. Of course,

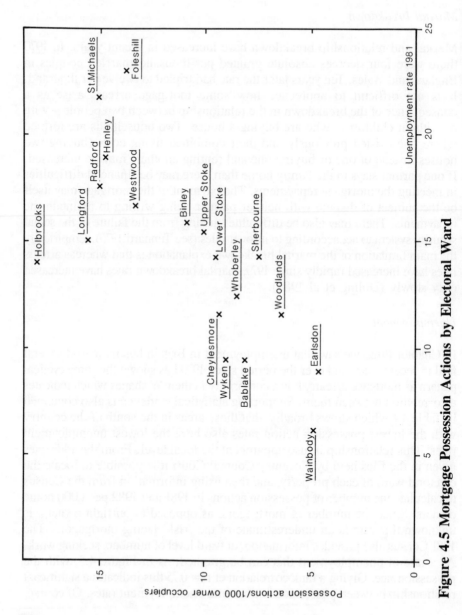

Figure 4.5 Mortgage Possession Actions by Electoral Ward

as with the longitudinal relationship between arrears and unemployment this does not establish that unemployment leads to possession proceedings in all or indeed in any of the cases. Although the correlations found are marked, establishing the existence of correlation is not the same thing as establishing causation. Both arrears and unemployment may be related to some third factor at present unidentified. Or, unemployment may be but one element of the wider phenomenon of labour market changes so that elements such as the loss of overtime earnings or short time working may more frequently lead to arrears. Nevertheless there is an obvious link between the trends, simply because unemployment invariably means lower income and a reduced ability to maintain previous expenditure patterns. As indicated in Chapter three the supplementary benefit system counteracts this only partially.

Incomes and loan/income ratios

The ability of borrowers to cope with the two sorts of situation – falling incomes and increased costs – which Merrett (1982) identified as leading to arrears is, all other things being equal, reduced where income net of mortgage repayments is low. In other words when the household budget is already stretched freedom of action under the impact of external shocks is restricted. Income net of mortgage payments, will be low in two general situations: when the loan to income ratio is high, and when income is low. These two situations are discussed below.

It has long been the practice of lending institutions to give loans up to some multiple, say 2½ or 3 times, of the borrower's income. So a person earning £5,000 per year could borrow £15,000 whilst one earning £10,000 per year £30,000. This principle has been given statutory recognition by the Housing Act 1980 which gave those exercising their right to buy their council home, a right to a mortgage based on a fixed multiple of their income. A limitation of this approach is that it fails to recognise that the income, net of mortgage repayments may be so low for someone with a small gross income that they have very little margin for fluctuation in either income or necessary expenditure. In these circumstances, sickness, pregnancy, even temporary unemployment, unanticipated repairs, overcommitment on consumer credit, poor budgetting and increases in the interest rate are all more likely to lead to mortgage arrears. Ford (1984, p. 16) has identified a similar set of circumstances:

> 'Considering building society borrowers in general, there has been a sharp increase in the percentage of borrowers (essentially first time borrowers) receiving 100% loans, and this is clearly the case for those now in arrears. High percentage loans suggest that borrowers have little financial cushioning, either to invest in the property initially, or to act as a buffer against additional, financial demands, and low income clearly has a role in generating this situation'.

Thus the rapid growth in home ownership over the last decade has meant the recruitment of people from further down the income scale. Increasing numbers of home owners thus have few savings and limited spare income which they can use to get out of trouble. Wenzlick (1964) has argued that in the United States increasing rates of mortgage arrears are a necessary consequence of expanding home ownership to 'people who are marginal in their ability to pay for and maintain their homes' (p. 230). This does not mean that low income groups will necessarily miss mortgage payments but that by virtue of their income they are more susceptible to other factors which precipitate arrears. This fact itself means that it may be the precipitating factor – sickness or consumer credit – which is identified as a significant cause of arrears when they have actually done no more than to tip the delicately balanced budgetary scales. The corollary is that without that underlying instability many incidents would not lead to arrears.

This conclusion receives some support from the results of Ford's study in which she found that although mortgage arrears and possessions were experienced across the range of borrowers in terms of income, size of loan, age and occupation the majority of cases were 'concentrated amongst young, first time borrowers with high percentage loans' (Ford 1984, p. 28). Further support for the significance of low incomes as underlying much of the arrears is provided by a comparison with rent arrears where it has been found that

> 'tenants in serious arrears were financially worse off than tenants in the random sample. Where money is short, skilful management of household income is crucial if debt is to be avoided, and unexpected expense or a drop in income is likely to make the task more difficult' (Duncan and Kirby 1983, p. 51).

The extent to which, in order to enter home ownership, first time buyers have extended themselves financially is shown by Figure 4.6. Line A describes the ratio of the average loan to the average income of first time buyers with building society mortgages. Although the increase in this ratio from 1971 to 1973 can be seen to precede the 1974/75 peak in arrears of Figure 4.1, there is no corresponding increase proceeding the post 1979 peak in arrears. However, since the ratio does not take account of variation in the rate of interest charged on mortgages it is arguably a poor guide to the financial burden facing house buyers, when interest rates vary considerably as they did after 1978. In this respect a better measure is provided by line B. This has been calculated by assuming a twenty-five year repayment period on an average building society advance to first time buyers repaid at the BSA recommended rate of increase, all divided by the average gross income of first time buyers. The ratio has varied from a low point in 1971 when for the average first time buyer just over 18 per cent of gross income went on mortgage payments, to 1973 when

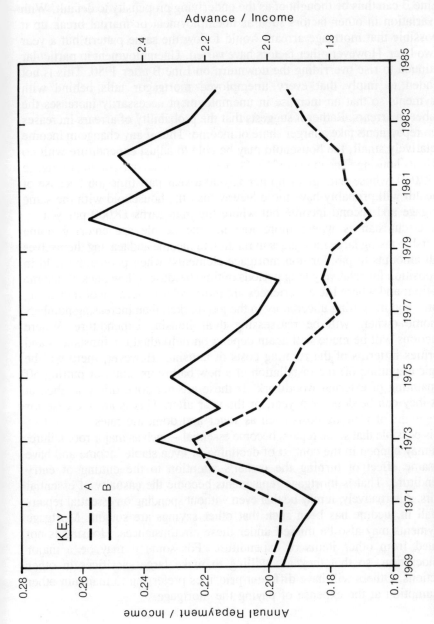

Figure 4.6 Repayment and Advance to Income Ratios

77

this rose to almost 24 per cent, falling back to 20 per cent in 1978, and increasing to 26 per cent in 1980. Although this has subsequently fallen back by 1984 it was still almost 22 per cent.

Line B can thus be thought of as the underlying propensity to default. With no variation in other factors such as unemployment or marital break up it is possible that mortgage arrears would follow the same pattern but a year or two later. However other factors have varied. Unemployment in particular continued to rise overriding the downturn on Line B after 1980. This is not intended to imply that every unemployed mortgagor falls behind with repayments so that an increase in unemployment necessarily increases the number in arrears. Rather it suggests that the probability of arrears increases when repayments take a larger share of income. Thus if any change in income is relatively small, the household may be able to adjust expenditure with no loss to its housing. The man on £40,000 per year with an outstanding mortgage of £10,000, whose wife gives up her £5,000 a year part-time job because of ill health will probably have more leeway than the household with the same mortgage and second income but where the man earns £8,000 per year.

In circumstances where more low income people are entering home ownership taking large mortgages in relation to income and leaving themselves small amounts to pay for non mortgage elements; when people are held in this position for relatively long periods of time because of low rates of income inflation; and where life experiences are more volatile because of increasing divorce and increasing uncertainty in the job market, then increasing numbers of home owners will be reassessing their housing expenditure. Where reductions will be made will again depend on individual circumstances and priorities in terms of the running costs of housing. However, there will be a logic to putting off the installation of a new bathroom suite, or putting off the painting of external woodwork. If these are not done this year then at least they can be done next year, or the year after. This is not the case for other items of running costs such as water and domestic rates.

It is possible that some repairs become essential – such as major roof failure. This may happen in the context of declining or even stable income and have the same effect of turning the owner's attention to the cutting of entry expenditure. That is mortgage repayments become the casualty of essential repairs. Alternatively, it may be that even without spending on essential repairs the fall in income has been such that other savings are sought. Mortgage repayments may also be missed under these circumstances. Housing is not isolated from other items of expenditure. For some it may be a major consideration, so that they are willing to make large sacrifices in other directions. Others will have different priorities preferring to maintain other consumption at the expense of paying the mortgage.

78

The consequences of arrears

Whilst, as we have seen, a variety of factors have contributed to the higher incidence of mortgage arrears, and this has posed a threat to the security of tenure of increasing numbers of home owners, we need to consider what this threat means in practice. The reality is certainly not that the threat is always carried through to realisation. The survey carried out by Ford and Took (1986) showed that fewer borrowers had 6 months arrears than had 5 months arrears, that fewer had five months arrears than had 4 months arrears, and so on. Our own survey of Coventry households established that some people who had previously been in arrears were no longer so and apparently managing to cope, successfully, with the entry costs of home ownership. So, for the individual, being in arrears at one point of time does not necessarily mean that they will be subsequently evicted.

There is, equally, evidence that the outcomes are not always a return to normal repayments. Table 4.1 shows that as the incidence of arrears has increased so has the numbers of borrowers facing mortgage possession actions in the county courts. Even these trends, however, do not mean that these borrowers necessarily lose their security of tenure in the sense of being evicted from their homes. Some of the borrowers faced with legal action will subsequently organize their affairs such that they are able to pay off their arrears and to return to normal repayments. In this present section we shall show how these various outcomes occur. At the same time routes, other than legal eviction following a mortgage possession action, to losing the home – that is experiencing actual insecurity of tenure – will also be identified.

Following the issue of a summons for possession and before case is heard before a county court registrar, there is a period of varying length in which a number of things can happen. The summons may prompt borrowers to reschedule debts to pay off a mortgage arrear rather than, say, the outstanding hire purchase; or they may borrow money from another source. Other borrowers may 'accept the inevitable' and hand over the keys to the lender, or put the house on the market. In some cases there will be negotiations between the parties to reach agreement about the repayment of arrears. Thus by the time that a case is heard some owners will have 'saved' their homes, some will have 'lost' them, leaving some for whom the issue remains in doubt. However unless the action is withdrawn the registrar is required to make a decision.

Examination of records in Coventry County Court in 1982 (see Doling et al 1984) showed that 9.2 per cent of the cases were withdrawn and 29.9 per cent were adjourned. These two types of decisions can be roughly equated with the case being settled, at least temporarily, prior to the hearing. For example the case may be withdrawn if the arrears have been cleared, and adjourned where an agreement has been reached by the two parties. Some cases, however, are adjourned because the court wants further information, for example, whether or not someone in a divorce case will receive legal aid. In these instances the case is not 'settled', but 'pending'. Nevertheless, in the remaining 60 per cent of cases the issue was unresolved at the time of the hearing. The registrars granted an outright possession in 17.1 per cent of the cases and a suspended possession in 43.6 per cent. Neither of these, however, necessarily imply a particular course of action. Again the borrower may, subject to circumstances, do a number of things from repaying the arrear to 'accepting the inevitable'. In order for the lender to take possession, where this is not voluntarily offered by the borrower, a warrant must be sought from the court. In Coventry this was done in about a quarter of all those cases in which a suspended or outright possession order was granted. Even after a warrant has been issued, however, the owner's situation may still be saved by paying off the arrear.

What this amounts to is that the actual number of home owners who lose their homes as a result of a mortgage possession action is unknown. Moreover, since unknown numbers of mortgagors 'voluntarily' sell their properties before a summons for a possession action is issued, and conceivably before (serious) arrears occur, the problems of arriving at a realistic estimate are even more intractable. Probably we can say little more than that some home owners do give up, or have taken away, their homes as a result of mortgage repayment difficulties. The numbers are unknown but are probably proportional to trends in mortgage arrears. In other words as arrears rise then so will all the other symptoms of financial difficulty though not necessarily on a one to one basis.

Knowledge of what happens to people subsequently is also scanty, and for the same reason. Longitudinal studies of representative cross sections of households are required in order to trace their housing position, changes to it and the determinants of change. In the absence of this we are reduced to inferences from aggregated and cross sectional data and to anecdotal evidence. The survey of Coventry County Court files gives some indication of the financial constraints limiting the ability of borrowers to sell their present homes and from their accumulated equity purchase outright another one further down the housing market. Where the house was already at or close to the bottom of the housing market it might be suggested that they had nowhere further down market to go. This was the position for 90 of the 462 properties (19.5 per cent) which were the subject of a possession action in 1982. A further 122 properties (26.4 per cent) were further up-market but since they had been purchased within the previous 4 years they may, depending on the percentage advance, have insufficient equity to purchase down market. In any case for those moving out of one house because of low income or unemployment many might have been better off by going into the rental sector. At least under housing benefit scheme they might have had their housing costs paid in full.

Of those which did not purchase another house, some may have gone into the private rental sector or to live with friends or relatives. Some may have turned to the council sector. Over the period from the last quarter of 1982 to the first quarter of 1985 about 7 per cent of those whom Coventry housing department rehoused under the homeless persons legislation were homeless because of mortgage default.

Conclusion

The body of empirical knowledge about mortgage arrears is scanty and diffuse. It does, nevertheless, point a number of conclusions about the failure to meet the entry costs of home ownership. Firstly, the incidence of arrears, together with the large proportionate increase in their incidence over the period since 1979, is such that the failure cannot be thought of as a minor or residual one. Short and long term failure to meet entry costs has become a widespread feature of home ownership. At any one time perhaps 5 per cent of borrowers are in arrears, with a higher percentage having been in arrears at some time since purchase. Arrears, therefore, have now become a feature of home ownership which many new home owners must, realistically, expect to face.

Secondly, there are indications from the available data concerning the reasons why arrears have come to take this relatively prominent position within the experience of home ownership. Unemployment and related phenomena, such as loss of overtime earnings, seem to have played a role. The long term financial commitment entailed in taking a mortgage is, under present circumstances, not well served by a labour market which for many cannot offer the long term security of the means of repayment. Other trends, particularly in marital and relationship breakup, have also contributed to mortgage arrears. But much of the evidence indicates a more general factor in the extension of home ownership to groups of the population who are marginal to the tenure. Arrears are particularly prevalent amongst young, first-time buyers who have borrowed to the limit in order to get a foot on the ladder. To this extent arrears are the consequence of, or price to be paid for, extending the tenure to marginal groups and perhaps indicate a limit of the size of the tenure under existing circumstances. At a less contentious level, the trends in arrears indicate simply that faced with decisions about their expenditure patterns more and more households are being forced, or choose to, reduce, permanently or temporarily, the entry costs of home ownership.

Thirdly, there are implications for security of tenure. Clearly not all those who go into arrears subsequently lose their homes or indeed are in any real danger of doing so. Equally clearly getting a foot on the home ownership ladder is no guarantee of not slipping off again. Many people are evicted as a consequence of court action. Many, also, lose their homes as a 'voluntary' response to meeting present or impending financial difficulties. The point therefore is that just as arrears have become a feature of home ownership in Britain in the 1980s, then so has insecurity of tenure. This can no longer be thought of as the exclusive preserve of the tenant.

5 House Condition

In Chapter three a distinction was made between the entry costs and the running costs of home ownership. In the previous Chapter we have discussed difficulties which home owners have experienced in maintaining the former; in the present Chapter we turn to the latter. Specifically, our interest is in maintaining the quality of the home. Relative to the previous Chapter, however, our task is aided by the availability of both more systematic and comprehensive data mainly collected by government surveys, and also of research carried out over an extensive period of time. The trends and the reasons for them are thus more readily identified.

The basis for maintaining the quality through further investment in the fabric of the property is to be found in the processes by which homes become obsolescent. These processes have been discussed elsewhere (Nutt et al 1976; Medhurst and Lewis 1969), but two are particularly relevant here. The first, as mentioned in Chapter three, is that the component parts of buildings wear out at different rates. Some elements, such as the brickwork, may be little affected by the ravages of time; others, such as internal decoration, plumbing and heating systems, may wear out or be accidentally damaged more quickly. If the household is to maintain the quality of the physical construction of the house then from time to time fresh investments of capital will be required. The second process of obsolescence occurs where rising standards or expectations generally result in some older houses being deemed not to have the characteristics or facilities normally expected of a house. Thus Burnett (1978) has provided evidence that by the end of the nineteenth century most houses had solid-fuel ranges for cooking and heating water, and gas lighting but did not have bathrooms or inside toilets. A large proportion of the present housing stock was built in the last century and without modification would not conform with today's living standards.

Both these processes, then, can lead to circumstances where households, in order to maintain or improve the quality of their home, decide to replace existing, but outworn, capitals or to add new capitals. To that extent they might be thought of as entry costs, particularly in cases where the costs are met by extensions to a first mortgage or by a second mortgage. In reality, however, most improvement work is not financed in this way. According to a recent survey 17 per cent of home improvements were financed by building society loans, 17 per cent by loans from other sources, with the remainder being financed from income or savings (Building Societies Association 1986). Only in a minority of cases, therefore, can loan default be relevant. Moreover in policy terms house condition issues have generally been thought of quite distinctly from access issues.

The Chapter begins by presenting evidence of recent trends in the condition of the housing stock. In this section the initial concerns are about the reliability and validity of the available data. To what extent are they describing actual trends? Do they deceive or disguise? Following these considerations it sets the scene for establishing, in the rest of the Chapter, how far the evidence on trends can be understood in terms of low income home ownership, particularly where there have been employment changes, and how much to other factors.

Trends in house condition

Measures of change in the condition of the stock of housing in England are provided by the English House Condition Surveys (EHCS) carried out by the Department of the Environment. Based on samples of dwellings located throughout the country, they provide a source of statistical information about housing in 1967, 1971, 1976 and 1981. In both 1976 and 1981 the physical condition survey was accompanied by a social survey which was intended 'to gauge the characteristics and resources of households in different parts of the stock, their perceptions and intentions in relation to defects observed by the physical surveyors, and their record of carrying out works to their home over the last five years' (DOE 1983, p. 1).

The setting up of the 1967 survey was, in part, due to deficiencies in the then existing knowledge of house condition, which was based on local authority returns about the number of unfit dwellings. These were known to be incomplete. They did not cover all dwellings and some authorities, such as

Glasgow, recorded only the number of unfit dwellings that they could reasonably deal with in the next decade (Farthing 1974). The attempt to provide a more accurate assessment has not been entirely fulfilled however. The measures used by those carrying out the surveys have had a significant subjective element, and, in order to reduce measurement error, the DOE has, from survey to survey, modified its procedures and instructions to the environmental health officers who carry them out.

Of the measures of condition used in the EHCS the absence of one or more of the basic amenities – inside WC, fixed bath in a bathroom, wash basin, hot and cold water at three points, and a sink – is arguably the least problematic. It requires surveyors to record the presence or absence of phenomena – fixed bath, kitchen sink, etc. – which can be fairly unambiguously defined. An analysis by O'Dell (1980) has demonstrated that, overall, errors in the recording of basic amenities in the 1976 EHCS were not large (though neither were they zero).

The measures of unfitness and disrepair are more problematic. The statutory guidance is contained in the 1957 Housing Act:

'In determining for any purpose of this Act whether a house is unfit for human habitation, regard shall be had to its condition in respect of the following matters, that is to say:

(a) repair
(b) stability
(c) freedom from damp
(d) internal arrangement
(e) natural lighting
(f) ventilation
(g) water supply
(h) drainage and sanitary convenience
(i) facilities for preparation and cooking of food and for the disposal of waste water

and that a house shall be deemed to be unfit for human habitation if and only if it is so far defective in one or more of the said matters that it is not reasonably suitable for occupation in that condition.' (S4 Housing Act 1957).

The statutory definition of unfitness has been criticized as failing to provide 'a useful operational definition' so that ultimately 'reliance is put on the subjective judgement of an inspector with some statutory guidance in the matter' (Farthing 1975, p. 15).

The problem with the evaluation of disrepair is not so much the identification of what elements of a dwelling are in need of repair but the cost of those repairs. Differences in total repair costs for the stock as a whole, recorded by the 1967, 1971 and 1976 surveys, thus in part reflect the different methods used to cost disrepair. In the 1967 survey, the outstanding repair cost of a dwelling was an estimate, made by the surveyor on the spot, of the total cost of any necessary repairs. In the 1971 survey, however, surveyors were required to decide into which cost band each dwelling fell, and if this was over £250 to record also each element of repair work required, e.g. repainting, reroofing, repointing. This was amended again in 1976 when surveyors were required to record whether each building element required 'no action', 'minor', 'medium', or 'major' repairs, or 'complete renewal'. The repair cost of each element was based on costs of rebuilding a 'standard' house: a three bedroomed terraced house of 70-80 square metres, but adjusted for the size of the dwelling in question. The total repair cost was the summation of the repair costs of the individual elements.

The report of the 1981 EHCS suggested that this procedure had led to an underestimate of the actual repair costs in 1976. This arose because, firstly, surveyors frequently assumed that dwellings had 'the nominal floor area of 70-80 square metres when they were in reality larger' (DOE 1982, p. 36). Secondly, many of the buildings in substantial repair actually had higher unit repair costs than the standard house. The 1981 survey accommodated these problems by following the procedures developed in the 1979 Greater London House Condition Survey. In this a number of standard houses were identified each with its own cost structure. The disrepair cost of each dwelling surveyed was then estimated on the basis of the particular standard house which it resembled. These cost models were modified for: size; whether the house was detached, semi-detached or terraced; where there was double counting e.g. scaffolding would be used for repairs to two or more elements; and where economies of scale could be achieved (GLC 1981).

The consequences of changing the methodology between surveys is that apparent trends in the results may owe more to differences in methodology than to real changes and this makes the identification of the real trend difficult. In the analysis of the 1981 survey, however, there was an attempt to reassess the results of the 1971 and 1976 surveys so that all three were compatible. Table 5.1 shows that this reassessment resulted in some relatively minor changes in the estimates of dwellings lacking at least one of the basic amenities. The changes in the number of dwellings unfit for human habitation in 1976, however, was considerable representing an increase in the estimate by 46 per cent. The effect of these changes has been to make the progress in reducing the number of dwellings without amenities appear better; and to give the impression that the number of unfit dwellings has not increased. Thus without the amendment to the 1976 survey the results would have indicated rather than a 4 per cent decrease in the number of unfit dwellings over the period 1976 to 1981, a 41 per cent increase. Matthews (1983) has argued that these results contradict usual

assumptions about the way in which house condition has changed, but that
the lack of explanation in the survey report inevitably casts doubt on our
understanding of what has actually changed.

Table 5.1 Changes in House Condition Assessments

(000's)

Year	1976 Survey	1981 Survey
Number of dwellings lacking at least one of the basic amenities		
1971	2,655	2,815
1976	1,493	1,531
1981	–	910
Number of dwellings unfit for human habitation		
1971	1,147	1,216
1976	794	1,162
1981	–	1,116

Source: DOE (1982).

The position on changes in disrepair is also uncertain. The uncertainty stems
from the fact that although the 1971 and 1976 surveys provided estimates
of the total cost of outstanding repairs for the stock as a whole the 1981 survey
did not. It is possible to estimate, from the information given about the number
of dwellings requiring repairs in each cost band, however, that the national
cost of outstanding repairs is £35.4 billion, but changes in the methodology
make it impossible to compare this figure with the earlier figures. Comparisons
are restricted to the DOE's own conclusion that the total number of 'dwellings

in serious disrepair [repairs costing £7000 and over] increased by about 200,000 between 1976 and 1981 and represented an increase in 22 per cent on the 1976 figure' (DOE 1982, p. 12).

Doubts about the accuracy of estimates of changes in condition over time necessarily raises doubts about the accuracy of any one of the surveys. If the 1976 survey was inaccurate then can we be sure that the 1981 survey is also not inaccurate? In practice the dearth of any systematic and comprehensive surveys largely reduces the exercise of examining the present position either to abandoning the attempt or to accepting the figures at face value, albeit with caution and backed up when possible by other evidence. Taking the latter approach it is evident that in 1981 there was considerable disrepair within the home owner stock. The survey presented information about the number of dwellings in each tenure which required repairs in each of seven cost bands. Making assumptions about mid-points it is possible to derive the estimates in Table 5.2. This shows that although dwellings in the private rental sector and those vacant had the highest average repair costs, they constituted only 15 per cent of the stock. The major incidence of disrepair lay in the home ownership sector, not just because of its large proportion of the stock but also because of its high average cost of disrepair. Despite the conventional wisdom that home owners have vested interests in maintaining the physical condition of their homes, the survey shows that many home owners do not make sufficient investments to bring their properties to a standard considered satisfactory according to DOE criteria. Similarly not all home owners have invested sufficiently to provide themselves with the five basic amenities (3.3 per cent lacked at least one) or to make their homes fit (4.7 per cent were unfit). High standards of quality, as measured by the house condition surveys, are thus not universal within home ownership.

Further evidence in the 1981 survey report points to significant variations within the sector. Owners of houses constructed before 1919, for example, had disrepair costed at an average of about £3,800 whilst 12.9 per cent of these houses were deemed unfit and 8.5 per cent lacked one or more of the basic amenities. The corresponding figure for owners in houses constructed after 1945 were a disrepair bill of £680, with no unfit dwellings and 0.8 per cent lacking amenities. Not only was the condition of the housing very different, however, but so was the remedial action which was being taken. Indeed the housing in worst condition (often though not always built before 1919) tended to have the poorest owners and the least amount of money spent on the properties. Conversely the housing in the best condition to start with had most spent on it. Home owners of property built after 1945, for example, spent on average 'twice as much ... as was needed to remedy the type of defect identified in the survey' (DOE 1983, p. 3). According to the criteria of the survey, therefore, the picture was of some home owners who were 'under-investing' with others 'over-investing'.

Table 5.2 Cost of Outstanding Repairs by Tenure

Tenure	Average cost per dwelling (£)	No. of dwellings (000's)	% of total dwellings (%)	Total repair cost (£b)	% of total repair cost (%)
Home ownership	1,883	10,297	57	19.4	54.8
Local authority	1,228	5,056	28	6.2	17.6
Privately rented	3,559	2,087	12	7.4	21.0
Vacant	3,727	626	3	2.3	6.6
All dwellings	1,957	18,066	100	35.4	100

Source: Estimated from DOE (1982) Table 21.

The evidence of the 1981 English House Condition Survey is, then, that there appears to have been a long term improvement in the quality of the home owner stock, though there may also have been a deterioration in the last five year period. In addition, the condition of the stock is variable with both high and low quality owner occupied houses: newer, well-maintained housing which had had more repairs and maintenance expenditure than was warranted by their levels of disrepair alone, as against older, badly maintained housing which had had less repair expenditure. With respect to basic amenities both these conclusions are supported by the Census. Table 5.3 shows that there had been a decrease, between 1971 and 1981, in the proportion of houses in home ownership in England which lacked a fixed bath or shower, or an inside WC. Also consistent with the house condition survey is the variation between the top and bottom ends of the market. In the enumeration districts corresponding roughly with our study areas Mount Nod had no dwellings lacking an inside WC in 1971, whereas a third of Hillfields home owners did.

Table 5.3 Proportion of the Owner Occupied Stock Lacking Amenities by Area

	Lacking fixed bath or shower		Lacking inside wc	
	1971	1981	1971	1981
Mount Nod	0.2	0.0	0.0	0.0
Allesley Park	0.1	0.0	0.0	0.0
Cheylesmore	0.1	0.05	5.2	1.1
Poets Corner	0.2	0.1	3.1	0.6
Radford	0.1	0.2	7.4	2.2
Holbrooks	2.0	0.1	23.8	4.1
Charterhouse	12.5	3.1	17.2	5.1
Hillfields	32.2	5.7	33.0	6.5
Coventry	5.4	0.9	8.2	1.8
England	5.7	1.5	7.8	1.9

Source: Office of Population Censuses and Surveys, Census 1971 and Census 1981.

In the rest of this Chapter there is an attempt to establish the extent to which these trends can be understood in terms of low income and our earlier deliberations about expenditure reductions in the area of running costs. We face, however, a major analytical problem in the form of confounding variables, so that it is difficult to isolate out the effects of income from the effects of other variables. Specifically, in the course of the Chapter we identify three sets of confounding variables: government policy with respect to urban renewal; household characteristics other than income; and market incentives. These form the focus of the three main sections which comprise the rest of the present Chapter.

The influence of government policy

The improvement in the condition of the home owner stock can, perhaps, be associated with increases in the real incomes of home owners. The argument would be that some share of national economic growth in post war Britain has been passed on to individual home owners who, in turn, have used some of that increase to demand higher levels of housing quality. It is not the intention here to pursue such an hypothesis but rather to note that later in this Chapter the variability in condition can be attributed, in part, to variations in income. Initially we will concentrate on the extent to which government policies on slum clearance and rehabilitation have contributed to improvements. This also acts as one of the bases for considering the varying state of disrepair of the housing stock.

Slum clearance

Central government legislation directed at the improvement of the standard of the housing stock has a long history. Acts of Parliament in 1868 and 1875 gave local authorities powers to demolish unsafe or insanitary housing although the adoption of these powers received scant encouragement from central government and, in practice, they were seldom implemented. The first major adoption of the slum clearance approach came with the Greenwood Act in 1930 which enabled local authorities to deal with slums by declaring clearance areas: and during the period between 1931 and 1938 about 300,000 houses were demolished. In the immediate post war period , however, the emphasis was placed on house building in an effort to make up the shortage in numbers and it was not until inroads had been made into that shortage, that considerations of quality were reemphasised. From the mid 1950s local authorities reinstituted slum clearance programmes and built new council houses for those displaced. The impetus for this came, initially, with the Housing (Rent and Repairs) Act 1954. Two years later subsidies for general needs housing were abolished leaving only those for slum clearance. This gave local authorities further encouragement to pursue slum clearance.

The crux of the approach was that local authorities surveyed the districts for which they were responsible and established which houses were unfit for human habitation. If it was deemed that the most satisfactory response was that the dwellings should be demolished, that the local authority could find suitable alternative accommodation for those displaced by the demolition and that it had sufficient resources to achieve these ends, then the local authority could designate Clearance Areas. The legislation also provided the procedures whereby local authorities could compulsorily purchase the properties to be cleared. In practice it came to mean that many local authorities cleared large tracts of houses and other buildings within their boundaries, frequently replacing them with new council housing on the same tracts. This process of comprehensive redevelopment resulted in fundamental change in 'massive inner areas of all the major cities and towns of Britain' (Paris and Blackaby 1979, p. 11). By the end of the 1950s local authorities were demolishing 60,000 dwellings per year, a level which continued until the mid 1960s, rising to 70,000 dwellings in 1967 and then falling again to the 60,000 per year level.

Although in earlier years the comprehensive redevelopment approach to urban renewal received generally enthusiatic support a number of writers (eg. Paris and Blackaby 1979; and Gibson and Langstaff 1982) have argued that from the mid 1960s this enthusiasm began to wane. Firstly, doubts about the economic burden incurred by local authorities begin to grow. Although throughout the 1950s and early 1960s the British economy expanded, albeit at a fluctuating rate, it did at least expand, so that expensive as large scale comprehensive redevelopment was the economy was perceived as being able to cope. From the mid 1960s, however, economic growth slowed down and public sector initiatives generally, being based on assumptions of continued growth, were called into question. Increasingly comprehensive redevelopment came to be seen as imposing a burden which the country could not afford. Secondly, there was growing concern in some quarters about the tenure implications of this activity. Redevelopment meant increasing the size of the public housing sector. At first the consequences of this were limited because it was expanding at the expense of the private rental sector. As the very worst areas were cleared, however, it increasingly came to mean that it was at the expense of owner occupied housing. This was certainly not in line with the ideological predilections of the political Right, but it also met with fierce resistance from many of the owners involved. Council housing might have been a prize for the private tenant, but for the home owner it was more likely to be considered a retrograde step. Finally, there was growing awareness of the social problems associated with comprehensive redevelopment. Academic studies, such as Wilmott and Young's classic study of Bethnal Green (Wilmott and Young 1962), as well as studies by others such as Shelter (Gee 1975), highlighted the consequences, some of them adverse, of both the process and outcome of redevelopment and rehousing.

There was, however, an alternative. In the post war period a second approach to improving the housing stock has received increasing support and after 1974 it came to be the dominant approach. The rehabilitation, rather than clearance, of unsatisfactory private housing first obtained government support in 1949. By an Act of that year, if a residential property could, generally by the installation of basic amenities, be given a future life of a further thirty years local authorities were empowered to provide a grant to the owner of 50 per cent of the cost incurred up to a maximum allowable cost of £600. The new scheme was not a numerical success partly because each individual grant required ministerial approval, but it did set a precedent and a framework which was to be built upon. The Housing (Rent and Repairs) Act 1954 which had reintroduced slum clearance made the grants both easier to obtain and more generous. As a result the take up of grants soon increased to over 30,000 per year.

Although legislation in 1959 introduced a further type of grant - the Standard Grant – neither rehabilitation nor comprehensive redevelopment were eradicating unsatisfactory housing quickly enough. Returns by the local authorities seemed to indicate that in 1965 there were only just over 800,000 unfit houses nationally, but two years later the 1967 National House Condition Survey estimated that the number was actually more than twice that, at about 1,800,000. The fact that this figure was so high despite the clearance of nearly three quarters of a million homes in the previous twelve years, combined with the growing disillusionment with comprehensive redevelopment, was a forerunner to a redistribution of resources in favour of rehabilitation.

The Housing Act 1969 which followed introduced a new concept in the form of the General Improvement Area (GIA). Local authorities were empowered to declare GIAs where they considered that living conditions could be enhanced by improvement of the environment of the area and/or its dwellings. The main emphasis was thus on physical condition. For individual owners the direct benefits of GIA designation were limited. Local authorities were able to spend up to £100 per house on environmental improvements, but owners themselves received no preferential treatment as far as grants were concerned. Perhaps the main advantage of declaration was that it was a statement by the local authority, at the same time as it was still carrying out slum clearance elsewhere, of its commitment to the future of the area. For many owners, therefore, GIA declaration was to be welcomed as an escape from the bulldozer.

The 1969 Act also extended the scope of the grant system making it applicable to the costs of repair undertaken as part of any improvement. This principle was taken further by the Housing Act 1974 which introduced a repair only grant. What had taken place, therefore, was an 'acceptance that owner-occupiers should be helped with the accumulated problems of disrepair' and that 'government has increasingly been prepared to extend subsidies to owners for works of both improvement and repair of property – once considered to be their sole responsibility' (Doling and Thomas 1982, p.241). It was a salutary indicator of the unwillingness or inability of home owners to maintain their homes even to the very minimum standards defined by longstanding legislation. Prosperity amongst home owners was still widespread, and home ownership itself had as yet spread only thinly down the socio economic scale, but even at this time pride in home ownership had not always led to the refurbishment of physical structure. Central government found it necessary, for whatever reason, to step in to support the market.

The 1974 Act, however, heralded other, equally significant, changes. Firstly it established rehabilitation as the principal policy to combat poor housing conditions. Comprehensive redevelopment was to go rapidly into decline and, in its place, rehabilitation was encouraged. Secondly, the Act introduced another approach to area based renewal. Housing Action Areas (HAAs) were intended for those areas which previously might, by virtue of their poor physical and social characteristics, have been considered as appropriate for comprehensive redevelopment. The aim was that living conditions would be significantly improved as a result of intensive local authority activity over a period of a maximum of five years. To assist in this aim owners were eligible for grants of 75 per cent of allowable costs, rising to 90 per cent in cases of hardship. Local authorities had powers to require landlords to improve their property, and, if necessary, to purchase and improve the property themselves. The Act also gave them powers to require home owners to improve their property. The Act thus firmly established grant-based rehabilitation as the principal approach to urban renewal giving local authorities real powers to begin to tackle the problems of renovating residential property.

The take up of grants in practice varied considerably from year to year. Table 5.4 shows that for England as a whole grants to private owners increased after 1969 to reach a peak of almost 200,000 grants in 1974, falling after that to under a third of the peak. As Gibson and Langstaff (1982, p. 116) put it: 'In "numbers game" terms the 1974-9 period was dismal'. In the first half of the 1980s however there has been a second peak exceeding in size that of the first.

Urban renewal in Coventry

The implementation of national urban renewal policy in Coventry, as elsewhere, has had a varying impact on the housing market. It has affected the scale and, through the channelling of grants to designated areas and to houses built

94

Table 5.4 Renovation Grants Paid to Private Owners

	England[a]	Coventry[b]
1970	71,293	767
1971	90,867	944
1972	124,176	1,649
1973	165,958	1,957
1974	192,348	1,272
1975	85,393	757
1976	68,718	523
1977	56,955	394
1978	57,578	420
1979	65,359	433
1980	74,465	526
1981	69,941	620
1982	104,028	905
1983	219,832	906
1984	229,097	900

(a) Fiscal years

(b) Calendar years

Sources: Housing and Construction Statistics; City of Coventry Environmental
Health Department.

before a certain time, the location of repair and improvement. Although the overall impact has been wide ranging the result has not, however, been the disappearance from Coventry of ill-maintained, unimproved and unfit housing.

The City of Coventry began to prepare its slum clearance plans ahead of central government legislation. The Development Plan which was prepared in 1951, though not approved until 1957, incorporated two Comprehensive Development Areas (CDAs): Spon End and Hillfields. Over the next decade there were proposals for further CDAs, although not all received Secretary of State approval. Only Hillfields CDA and its extension overlaps with any of our eight study areas. In 1961, four years after approval, Hillfields CDA still contained 2,199 dwellings in which 5,600 people lived. It was anticipated that within the following five years over half the houses would probably be declared as unfit for human habitation. The proposed pace of clearance and rebuilding, however, was a slow one with completion anticipated only by 1980 (City of Coventry 1961). Slow progress indeed proved to be the case. The Council reported in 1972 that '20 years after their original inclusion in the [Development] Plan large areas are still being acquired and substantial redevelopment has still [to] be carried out' (City of Coventry 1972, p. 2).

From the 1960s, however, Coventry also had an explicit policy of using grants to promote repairs and improvement. Although the intention was that clearance and redevelopment were appropriate where dwellings were unfit or obsolete, it was also recognised that despite the 'large scale redevelopment programme envisaged for the next fifteen years, there will still be many areas of substandard housing in the City' (City of Coventry 1966, p. 66). It was further recognised that 'much of this housing which, while lacking basic facilities, is not structurally unsound and could be improved' (p. 66). In line with this view the Council had indeed been making grants available so that over the decade from 1955/6 to 1964/65 the Council gave 7,592 grants.

Following the 1969 Act the City Council was also able to consider the GIA approach and eventually designated the Colchester Street/Winchester Street GIA which is located in the Hillfields study area (see Figure 5.1). It was further proposed that GIA's would be declared in areas, containing 8,500 houses, which had less severe housing problems but which required environmental works. In addition, the 10,500 dwellings in the worst areas of housing, but not deemed to require environmental improvement, would be dealt with by 'repair area' treatment. Here owners would be faced with both compulsory repair orders and encouragement to carry out improvements but there would be no environmental works.

Table 5.4 shows the number of renovation grants (including conversion, improvement, intermediate, special and repair grants) paid to private owners in Coventry for each year from 1970 to 1984. The pattern, closely following that for the country as a whole, can be roughly divided into three periods.

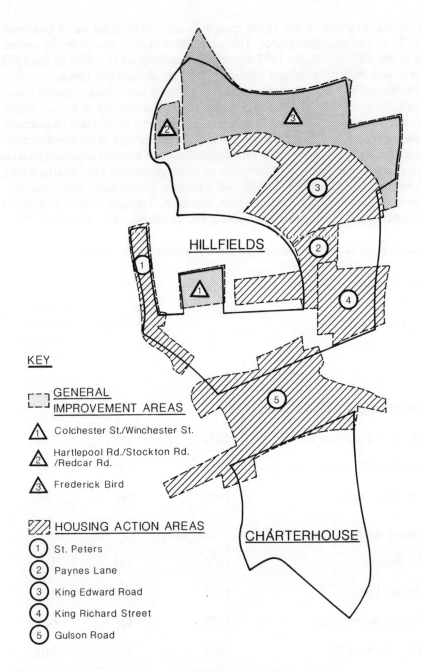

Figure 5.1 Renewal Areas in Hillfields and Charterhouse

97

During the first half of the 1970s grant take up was buoyant rising to a peak in 1973 of almost 2,000 grants. This was followed by a trough in the second half of the 1970s, with the 1977 figure only reaching about a fifth of the 1973 figure, and then by a second upturn in the first half of the 1980s.

The extent to which these area renewal policies have been successful can, in part, be gauged from Table 5.5 which shows the number of houses which have been improved. This level of success is due not only to intensive involvement of the local authority in encouraging grant take up but also to the involvement, in addition to home owners and private landlords, of housing associations who have taken a role in the improvement of older properties particularly within HAAs and GIAs. Thus by 1978, for example, six housing associations – Coventry Churches, New Hestia, Orbit, Stonham, Triangle Tenants Union and Viscount – had between them acquired 502 dwellings, and improved 287.

Table 5.5 Area Rehabilitation in the Hillfields Study Area

	Designated	Number of dwellings	Number of dwellings improved by 1984
General Improvement Areas			
Colchester St/Winchester St.	1971	158	153
Hartlepool/Redcar/Stockton	1974	140	132
Frederick Bird	1977	890	766
Housing Action Areas			
St. Peters	1976	129	112
Paynes Lane	1977	130	116
King Edward Road	1978	828	642
King Richard St.	1979	319	210

Although it followed from the fact of designating GIAs, HAAs and Repair Areas that grant take-up within them would be encouraged this did not mean that grants were confined to these areas. Indeed in some years, the majority of grants were taken up outside these areas. Increasingly however, the emphasis has been away from the unsystematic provision, largely in response to greater financial stringency on the Improvement Grant Capital Programme. By 1984 the demand for grants was double the number which could be met and council policy was that: 'Availability is at present restricted to mandatory grants, repairs grants in urban renewal areas, unfit houses and grants to disabled persons' (Coventry City Council 1984, para. 2.6.2(c)).

Household characteristics

Government policy, then, appears to have been instrumental both nationally and in Coventry in contributing towards long term improvement and repair of housing, particularly amongst the stock built before 1919. Notwithstanding this policy the state of disrepair of home owners' housing remains considerable though there is, in fact, a wide variation around the average. As we have indicated earlier, some home owners live in houses which are maintained to a high standard and which have all the basic amenities: others live in houses which lack amenities, are unfit and in a poor state of repair. In this section the objective is to look at this latter group and to explore some of the reasons why its members have not invested sufficiently to bring their homes to a standard which satisfies the criteria of the English house condition surveys.

The 1981 English house condition survey established correlations between, on the one hand, house condition, improvement and repair work, and, on the other hand, household characteristics. These show a strong association between unsatisfactory housing and low incomes and, to that extent, support hypotheses about limited ability to pay resulting in limited product quality. The correlations are not simply about income, however, but also about length of residence, family size and age of head of household (see Table 5.6).

Low income households The connection between unsatisfactory housing and low incomes has already been mentioned. Table 5.7 shows that nationally households in unsatisfactory dwellings are less likely to have heads in full time employment, and more likely to have retired heads. Median incomes also differ. Together these characteristics are both a cause, and a barrier to the improvement of unsatisfactory housing conditions. People buy housing in the poorest condition because they are poor, and then because they are poor face the largest financial difficulties in paying for repairs and improvements. The 1981 EHCS indicated that 64 per cent of those households in dwellings which were unfit and in serious disrepair faced costs of repair and improvement which were more than three times their annual household income.

99

Table 5.6 Household Expenditure by Home Owners on Renovation Compared with Average Household Expenditure in All Tenures (1976-1981)

	Ratio of household expenditure on renovation to average expenditure
Age of Head of Household:	
under 30	1.74
30-44	2.06
45-64	1.38
65 and over	0.82
Time at Present Address:	
under 3 years	3.13
3 to 5 years	1.79
6 or more years	1.13
Annual Income of Household Head:	
under £1820	0.64
£1821 to £4160	0.93
£4161 to £8840	1.56
£8841 or more	2.72
Type of Household:	
a individual under 60	1.04
b small adult	2.15
c small family	1.94
d large family	1.97
e large adult	1.43
f older small	1.03
g individual over 60	0.60

Source: DOE (1983) Table 38.

Table 5.7 Working Status of Head of Household by Condition

(Percentage)

	Satisfactory Dwellings	Unsatisfactory Dwellings				
		Fit			Unfit	
		All Amenities medium disrepair	Lacking amenities low/medium disrepair	Serious disrepair	Low/medium disrepair	Serious disrepair
Full time employment	62	56	34	53	46	38
Part time employment	4	4	3	5	4	2
Looking for work	4	5	3	4	6	6
Retired	22	25	45	27	30	38
Housewife/Other	8	10	15	11	14	16
All household	100	100	100	100	100	100
Median income head partner (£)	5566	3937	2238	4677	3077	2234

Source: DOE (1983)

The relationships indicated by the Coventry survey reflect this complexity. The *a priori* expectations of the association between income and renovation are indeterminate because although higher income people are better placed to pay for any necessary work, they are more likely to have used their buying power to purchase housing which required less work. In the Coventry survey most repair work was carried out by those in the middle income bands and least by those with lowest incomes (because they could not afford to?) and by those with highest incomes (because they did not need to?). The position with regard to improvements was different, however. Those on the lowest income (below £100 per week) had carried out the fewest number of improvements since purchasing their house. It might also be anticipated that the quality of improvements also differed by income. Another way of looking at the income-renovation relationship is with regard to the eight survey areas. The pattern for both improvements and repairs is that most work has been done by those households in the middle of the market, with little done at the bottom (Hillfields and Charterhouse) and at the top (Mount Nod and Allesley Park).

Length of residence The EHCS reported that households in unsatisfactory dwellings were more likely to have been in residence for a long time. Thus 51 per cent of residents of satisfactory dwellings had been residents for less than 10 years, and 7 per cent longer than 40 years. The corresponding proportions for those in dwellings which were unfit and in serious disrepair were 24 per cent and 29 per cent. One of the reasons for this is that renovation was often associated with a change of occupancy sometimes because this was a requirement of obtaining the mortgage.

Household type The EHCS also found associations at the national level between household type – defined by the size of the household and the age of its head – and renovation activity. One group of households which tend to carry out less renovation work is that headed by an elderly person. Donnison (1979, p. 48) has described their position:

'More and more of the pensioners are really elderly. Few of these people will be able to do their own major repairs to roofs, wiring, plumbing and paintwork. And for demographic reasons, fewer, as the years go by, will have children, nephews or grandchildren capable of helping them: for families have been growing smaller, generation by generation. So they depend increasingly on the labour-intensive jobbing builder whose costs have risen dramatically in recent years. The poorest pensioners were usually poorer than most when they were young. The poorest house-buyer tends to buy a cheaper house ... the only advantage the poorer house-buyer has – if indeed it is an advantage – is that those to whom he has to turn for loans are unlikely to impose on him any obligations to repair and repaint his house regularly. He could scarcely afford to anyway. But that means his home is more likely to become dilapidated later.'

Market processes

Although differential ability to pay would appear to be an obvious influence on the quantity and quality of products consumed, it is also important to consider why many households have not availed themselves of government subsidies in the form of repair and improvement grants. We shall argue here that this may also be a product, at least in part, of low incomes. There appears, however, to be a further type of influence, that of the incentives, or lack of them, provided by the market place. Both explanations are considered here.

The take up of grants In so far as repairs and improvement grants have been available it is pertinent to consider both why they have not been taken up more than they have and what their consequences for house condition have been. Here, it is convenient to start with the recognition that the declaration of renewal areas and the availability of grants has had differential consequences. In some areas the designations under the 1969 Act, in particular, proved to be the trigger mechanism whereby housing was upgraded physically. To that extent the legislation was meeting one of its stated objective of aiding the improvement of the housing stock. Sometimes, however, the areas were also upgraded socially. A process of gentrification took place, in areas such as Camden and Islington in London, where supply and demand factors meant that landlords could improve properties with the help of a local authority grant and then profit from increased rental and vacant possession values (Hamnett and Williams 1979). The outcome was, as Balchin (1985) amongst others has argued, not consistent with the apparent intention of directing subsidies towards those, generally low income people, living in poor housing:

> 'Improvement grants intended to benefit the residents of areas of substandard housing were manifestly not benefitting those residents. They were adding to the profit of developers, increasing the capital value of the properties of often non-resident landlords and helping to provide new homes for former commuters. Simultaneously communities were being destroyed as quickly as if major clearance schemes had been undertaken – many former residents doubling-up in increasingly multi-occupied dwellings, becoming homeless or moving elsewhere, often without trace.' (p. 73)

In other parts of the country, however, supply and demand factors have been quite different so that the outcomes of area renewal policies have also differed. In many GIAs and HAAs the main feature is the relatively low numerical level of grant aided improvement. Between 1969 and 1979 there were 1,293 GIAs declared throughout the country. These contained 410,006 dwellings of which 84,159 or 20.5 per cent received grants. Likewise of the 153,704 dwellings, in the 449 HAAs declared between 1975 and 1979, 21,689 (14.1 per cent) had received grants (Gibson and Langstaff 1982). The reality, then, is that most properties in designated renewal areas have not been improved, at least not with the aid of a local authority grant.

A number of authors (eg. Paris and Blackaby 1979; Monck with Lomas 1980; Watkins and Shutt 1980; and Doling 1986) have attempted to explain these low take up levels. One set of reasons appear to lie with the administrative hurdles involved in getting both the grant and the repair work carried out. Another barrier has been the rateable value limits set by the 1974 Act which restrict assistance to those properties with rateable values below £350 in Greater London and £175 elsewhere in the country. Thus in 1981 0.9 million of the 3.7 million homes which were unsatisfactory were excluded by virtue of their rateable values or date of construction (DOE 1983). The reasons for the low rate of improvement in areas declared as GIAs and HAAs are also to be found in the very reasons which led to their declaration. There is a marked statistical relationship between poverty and poor housing conditions which is based on the inability of the poor to compete successfully for better quality and more highly priced housing. Once lower income people become home owners, or if they become low income after they enter the tenure, one response, as we argued in Chapter three, is to neglect repairs and maintenance work. It was because of this general tendency that the findings of the 1981 English House Condition survey showed that households in unsatisfactory housing had lower incomes, were less likely to be headed by someone in full time employment, were more likely to be retired, more likely to be looking for work, and more likely to be headed by a woman, than those in satisfactory housing (DOE 1983). The same survey provides an indication of the cost of installing missing amenities and carrying out repairs in relation to annual household incomes. For those in dwellings which were satisfactory the median cost to annual income percentage was 4.5 per cent; for those in dwellings which were fit but in serious disrepair the median was 210 per cent; and for those in dwellings which were unfit and in serious disrepair the median was over 300 per cent (DOE 1983).

In Coventry, as in many other locations, the nature of the housing was not of sufficient intrinsic merit to attract higher income buyers. The potential for gentrification in the Hillfield's GIAs and HAAs has been limited for a number of reasons. The houses are small and at high densities. Typically their internal layout is of two up and two down with a one, or two, storey wing at the back. Frequently lacking garages, often with no front garden, and small back gardens the market demand for such property in Coventry is not buoyant. The aspirations of the better off households has been typically directed at suburban semis. Moreover since Coventry is a relatively small city with many major employment foci scattered throughout the built up area there is no great premium on a central location.

A consequence of these supply and demand factors is that areas of unsatisfactory housing are also likely to be areas of lower income households. Although it may be argued that low incomes are precisely the rationale for making public money available to assist with the expenditure incurred in improvement, it may be argued further that in practice such a policy will be hindered where the net cost of improvement, that is the total cost less the grant, is still high in relation to income. In theory the 90 per cent grant payable in cases of hardship is directed at this problem but, in practice, it may only be partially successful. This is because the 90 per cent is 90 per cent of the total cost, only where the total cost is within a fixed, 'allowable' cost. In practice the cost of improving many dwellings, particularly those owned by poorer households, exceeds the allowable cost so that a 90 per cent grant may imply a net cost to the householder in excess of 10 per cent of the total cost. As a result even the net cost in relation to annual household income may be high. The 1981 English House Condition Survey, which referred to this net cost as the 'grant gap', provides some evidence on this. Of those home owners in dwellings which were fit but in serious disrepair, 43 per cent faced grant gaps in excess of the size of their annual household income (DOE 1983).

In addition to the disparity between household incomes and the costs of improvement, there is a further disparity in many areas between these costs and the resulting market values of the improved dwellings. It might be argued that in a perfect market the market value of an improved house would be equal to the market value of an unimproved house together with the costs incurred in improvement. In practice, however, this has frequently been found not to be the case. Harrison (1979), has referred to the 'valuation gap' as describing the situation where the costs of repair are not matched by a commensurate increase in market value so that in investment terms improvement costs may not be justified. In some instances not only may the total cost of repairs be a poor investment but, to the individual householder, so may the net cost.

Table 5.8 provides a numerical estimate of the size of valuation gaps in the three GIAs designated within our Hillfields study area. Although the figures are approximations they do indicate the order of magnitude of the valuation gaps in each area. These varied from area to area in 1974 being highest in the Colchester Street/Winchester Street GIA, but were equal across the GIAs in 1979. The valuation gaps in 1979, however, were much higher so that relatively the disincentive effect was greater than it was in 1974. This situation arose because whereas on the one hand the costs of improvement increased by over 50 per cent between 1974 and 1979, on the other hand the market values of both improved and unimproved properties increased by much smaller percentages.

The reasons for the existence of a valuation gap are not clear. It may be that repair work, because it is a one-off activity, does not share the economies of scale of new house production, or the process of repair may be inherently more difficult and time consuming than building *ab initio*. It may be that the market value of unimproved housing is bid up as a result of a relative scarcity of lower quality housing brought about by governmental imposition of minimum standards. Alternatively their market value may be bid up by those wishing to use their leisure time to carry out repairs themselves and applying a low or even negative cost to their time. Whatever the reason, or reasons, however, the market frequently does not provide incentives to improve dwellings. Rather, those people able and willing to meet the cost of an improved house may find a cheaper solution in moving to an already improved house in the same area or elsewhere.

Table 5.8 The Valuation Gap in Three General Improvement Areas

		Market value: Improved	Unimproved	Value of improvement	Median total cost of improvement	Valuation gap
C/W	1974	6250	4000	2250	3500	-1250
	1979	7500	5000	2500	5500	-3000
HRS	1974	7000	3750	3250	3500	-250
	1979	7000	4500	2500	5500	-3000
KRS	1974	6500	3750	2750	3500	-750
	1979	7500	5000	2500	5500	-3000

Source: Calculated from Appendix 9 Marlow, D. (1979).

Key:

C/W Colchester St./Winchester St.
HRS Hartlepool/Redcar/Stockton.
KRS Frederick Bird.

The nature of the housing market may act in another way to provide incentives not to incur improvement costs. Davis (1960) and Rothenberg (1967) have both argued that the externalities of improvement work result in a particular case of the Prisoner's Dilemma found in game theory (see Luce and Raiffa 1957). Their argument is that the market value of a dwelling is largely a product of the tone and character of the housing in the immediate vicinity, and that what any one individual owner does is largely irrelevant in terms of house prices. Market prices generally may be high if all or most of the properties in an area give the appearance of solidity and good maintenance, but for the individual there will be little gain if his is the only well maintained house. In fact gains for the individual will be highest where everyone else incurs the cost of improvement and maintenance, but he or she does not. Without collusion or central direction, therefore, the best strategy for each individual is to do nothing, and there may be a tendency for every individual not to maintain their homes.

These various counteracting tendencies are arguably founded in the contradictions of urban renewal policies in Britain. The point has been made by Paris and Blackaby (1979) that housing decay is one manifestation of wider processes, and not simply something to do with physical structures. Housing is not an indepenent variable, in other words, and therefore not amenable to improvement by housing policy alone. They see, as the central inadequacy, that rehabilitation is a market oriented form of intervention which seeks to stimulate market processes whilst not controlling the crucial market relations which are the causes of decay. Much the same point has been made by Kirwan and Martin (1972, p. 128):

'So long as poor housing is associated with a low level of effective demand in a market where the price of housing generally reflects directly the increase in average incomes, obsolescence and poor quality housing will continue to co-exist beside well maintained and high quality housing'.

The fact that there is inequality of market power has been recognised by rehabilitation policy in a superficial way only. Public subsidies to improve the physical structure, and the immediate neighbourhood, in which low income people live are likely, as we have described, to have two possible and alternative long term impacts. Firstly, where there is pent up demand for improved housing in a given location, rehabilitation will result in increased market prices in the area in comparison with other areas. The greater this relative increase the more likely that market prices will lead to a displacement of the low income occupants by higher income occupants. If they were owner occupiers then they, or their beneficiaries, will make a windfall gain of the increased market value, whereas tenants may receive no benefits. In so far as the underlying inequality of market power is left unaltered those households displaced may demand alternative sources of low quality housing. There may be an extent to which publicly aided improvement of the housing stock in one area may be balanced by privately induced deterioration in another area: a case of chasing the slums around.

The second outcome would be where the residents before and after refurbishment are the same, there being little or no displacement. In so far as low housing quality is a reflection of low incomes and inability to pay, the designation of GIAs or HAAs, and the giving of grants do nothing in themselves to turn low incomes into high incomes. The long term outcome, then, might be that renewal was followed by a period of deterioration of the physical structure until it reached a level consistent with their (unchanged) demand for housing services. The expectation might be that the experience of living in a well maintained house acted as a spur to keep the home in or close to that position. In reality however the lesson might be taken to be that there is no point in paying for repairs and maintenance out of income because sooner or later the council will come round with another grant. In such circumstances, therefore, rehabilitation might be perceived as essentially a holding operation.

Repairs v improvements In considering the trends in house condition, as well as its present variability, the attitudes of home owners towards disrepair are also significant. The choice of criteria defining satisfactory housing condition may differ as between the technical expert and the householder. In addition even if there is agreement on the criteria it does not follow that the actual condition of a house will be accurately evaluated. According to the social survey conducted as part of the 1981 house condition surveys amongst home owners whose dwellings had been adjudged 'unfit' and 'in serious disrepair' 6 per cent thought that they were 'Almost perfect', 29 per cent that they were 'Better than would be expected', and only 5 per cent that they were 'Very bad' (DOE 1983). Of course there may be elements within these responses of self justification for not carrying out repairs, or other influences such as an implicit recognition of income constraints, but they might also be taken as some evidence that many households are less concerned about the official criteria of satisfactory housing than is the state.

A similar conclusion may also be suggested by further findings from the social survey. These established that of the repairs actually carried out between 1976 and 1981 many were not essential. By essential repairs is meant 'items of work necessary to make a building wind and weatherproof, to overcome certain structural defects and to forestall further rapid deterioration' (DOE 1983, p. 8). Rather, amongst home owners large proportions, particularly those in newer dwellings, had carried out 'modernisation' and 'enhancement' work. The survey report went on to note that:

> 'This emphasis was even more apparent when the individual items of work are ranked according to their frequency. At the top of the list for each age band

was central heating, replacement bathroom and kitchen fitments, external windows (mainly double glazing) and electrical wiring. All five items relate to the amenities and the services of the building rather than to the basic fabric, and they impinge particularly on the comfort convenience and lifestyle of the occupants' (DOE 1983, p. 15).

Similar evidence emerged from the Coventry household survey, where the largest proportions of reported work were with respect to bathroom and kitchen modernisation. A number of the Coventry sample recognised that there were repairs which needed doing. Thus 61 of the 306 sampled (20 per cent) said that the window frames required replacement, 9 per cent that the external walls, 10 per cent the guttering, 8 per cent the roof, 5 per cent the damp proof course, and 5 per cent the electrical wiring. The most frequently given reason for not doing these repairs, which were perceived as being required, was 'can't afford'. This was said by about half, with a further 20 per cent – presumably those who used their own labour – saying that they lacked the time. However when these households who had not carried out repairs because of some such constraint, were examined further it was found that large numbers had carried out improvements – particularly kitchen and bathroom improvements. The conclusion that seems to be reinforced is that people worry first about life's comforts – what they consume from a house on a day to day basis, and place higher priority on these than on repairs and investment. When income or time are major constraints then improvements may be carried out first with repairs put off to be completed at a later date.

It could be a mistake to interpret these findings solely in terms of the individuals' assessments of comfort. It may be that the market rewards one type of investment rather more than it favours another type. The rate of return, measured by an increase in capital value, may be higher per pound of investment in modernisation than in repairs. A test of this hypothesis is provided by attempting to explain the capital growth experienced by individual home owners in terms of a number of variables including whether or not they had carried out certain repair or modernisation work.

This can be carried out using multiple regression with a dependent variable (R_i) defined as:

$$R_i = \frac{P_{i1985}}{P_{in}} \cdot \frac{H_{1985}}{H_n}$$

where P_{i1985} = market value of house i in 1985, as perceived by owner

$$P_{in} = \text{purchase price of house i actually paid in year n}$$

$$H_{1985} = \text{average purchase price of all houses bought in the country in 1985}$$

$$H_n = \text{national average purchase price of houses in year n}$$

The dependent variable thus measures the ratio of the perceived increase in the value of a house to the average of actual increases in all houses purchased in the same year. Values greater than unity indicate that house i has performed better, in price terms, than the average; and values below unity that its performance has been worse (see Table 5.9).

The independent variables which are all dummies, can be grouped into 3 categories (see Table 5.9):

(i)   The location of house i. In line with the discussion in the next Chapter, this variable can be considered a proxy for a number of influences on house price including local unemployment levels, government subsidized rehabilitation, as well as access to local public goods.

(ii)   Improvements to house i. These are specific improvements or additions to amenities and fittings carried out since purchase.

(iii) Repairs to house i. These are specific repairs carried out since purchase.

The statistical procedure adopted was forward stepwise regression the results of which have been recorded, in Table 5.10, up to the step beyond which the variable to be added at the next step would not be significant at the 10 per cent level. The six variables included, collectively, provide a regression equation which is significant on the F test, and explains about 20 per cent of the variation in house price gains.

Perhaps of more interest, however, is the make-up of the six variables included. The two location variables – Mount Nod and Holbrooks – represent the top and the bottom ends of the market respectively. With the former having a positive coefficient and the latter a negative one they correctly reflect the increasing divergence in prices since 1980 which is discussed in the next Chapter. Of the possible repair variables only one – chimney – has a significant first order correlation. In fact, this variable is strongly correlated with work done to the gutters ($r = 0.515$), external walls ($r = 0.359$) and the main roof ($r = 0.329$), so that its inclusion may be partly on their account.

Although only one of the possible seven repair variables is included, three of the six improvement variables are, namely a new or replaced kitchen,

Table 5.9 First Order Correlation Coefficients

	Annual rate of house price increase as ratio of national average rate of increase

Survey Areas

Mount Nod	0.228
Allesley Park	0.050
Cheylesmore	0.074
Poets Corner	-0.027
Holbrooks	-0.245
Charterhouse	-0.124
Hillfields	0.045

Improvements

Bathroom	0.202
Kitchen	0.171
Central Heating	0.187
Double Glazing	-0.021
Loft Insulation	0.025
Garage	0.145

Repairs

Chimney	0.195
Gutters	0.131
External Walls	0.142
Main Roof	0.150
Window Frames	0.111
Plasterwork	0.086
Electrical Wiring	0.118

Table 5.10 Relative House Price Gains

Independent variables	Coefficients (t-stats)
Holbrooks	-0.1044 (3.743)**
Kitchen	0.0423 (2.2072)**
Mount Nod	0.0808 (3.201)**
Chimney	0.0762 (2.391)**
Central heating	0.0478 (2.062)**
Bathroom	0.0353 (1.807)*
R	0.446**

** Significant at the 5 per cent level
* Significant at the 10 per cent level

bathroom and central heating system. The actual level, quality and therefore cost of the work done will have varied from house to house. However, it might be argued that the inclusion of all three is a reflection of the relative importance of improvements as opposed to repairs in determining price gains. This would be important whether the element P_{i1985} in the dependent variable was perceived accurately or whether it differed greatly from actual market value. In the former case it would demonstrate that the market did indeed react in a certain way to individual supply side changes, whilst in the latter it would demonstrate that in fact people believe that the reaction would be in that certain way. In terms of their own perceptions the home owners are behaving rationally in deciding to invest in modernisation rather than repairs.

Conclusion

In this Chapter we have attempted to establish the extent to which home owners have reduced their expenditure on running costs, especially repairs and maintenance. The evidence of the surveys of house condition in England indicates that whereas there has been a long term improvement in the standard – measured by amenities and fitness criteria – of the houses of home owners, recently there seems to have been a deterioration in their state of repair. In addition, there appear to be two distinct groups of owner: those who spend money on repairs and those who do not. For present purposes the research problem becomes that of trying to establish why the trends are as they are and especially why the non repairers are non repairers. Given our considerations, the role of income in these explorations is clearly central.

The Chapter has identified a number of influences. Government policy on urban renewal has contributed to increasing housing standards as well as assisting the repair of many homes. The assistance has been differential however. It has been mainly targetted on older housing with disrepair in newer housing often unaided. But not all old houses have been the object of government help, and neither have all old houses in poor repair. The nature of the housing market is also important because of the evidence that it can send signals, in the form of prices, which may act as a disincentive to expenditure on repairs and maintenance. There appear to be several facets to this but one consequence appears to be that modernisation and upgrading is encouraged, sometimes at the expense of repairs. Another is that the signals may frustrate the impact of renewal policies.

In addition to these influences household characteristics, including both income and other characteristics, seem to be related to disrepair. Households with the lowest incomes tend to purchase the cheapest housing and that is frequently in the worst state of repair. They then have the least ability to meet running costs. Households who become low income owners, after purchase, may also experience difficulties in meeting repair costs. They can be seen as lowering the quality of their housing to make it more consistent with their lower incomes. Overall, however, the conclusion might be that although low incomes help to explain the lack of expenditure on repairs and maintenance there are also other influences. Of major significance are the ways in which the market structures, or influences, individual decision making.

6 House Prices

Chapters four and five concentrated on the expenditure behaviour of individuals in line with our earlier deliberations about the entry and running costs of home ownership. In this Chapter we move from the individual to the market. Its concern is with the market outcomes, in terms of price trends, which result from concentrations of home owners who have low incomes. More narrowly, it examines the impact of unemployment on price trajectories. As in previous Chapters, empirical evidence is presented at different levels of aggregation.

National house price trends

Over the period from 1954 to 1984 average house prices in the UK increased by over sixteen times. This increase has not been smooth, however. From Table 6.1 it is possible to show that in the 1950s annual increases were of the order of 3 per cent, rising in the 1960s to about 7 per cent. During the 1970s the rate of change both accelerated and fluctuated wildly. In 1972 alone average prices increased by 42.4 per cent, in 1978 they rose by 26.2 per cent, and in 1979 by 29.3 per cent but in 1974 they rose by under 5 per cent. Over the whole period the average earnings in all occupations together increased by about the same factor. Although there have been large divergences between the two trends taken on a year by year basis, in the long term they have been broadly associated.

    The house price index in Table 6.1 can be viewed as a measure of the investment performance of home ownership. Whilst over the whole of the post war period up until the end of the 1970s house prices had increased by a factor of sixteen, and retail prices by a factor of nine, share prices increased only five fold (Kilroy 1979). Depending upon location, quality and year of

Table 6.1 Inflation in Prices and Incomes

	Average house price £	House price index	Retail price index	Index average earnings
1954	1,990	100	100	100
1955	2,080	105	104	109
1956	2,150	108	107	115
1957	2,180	110	114	122
1958	2,220	112	116	124
1959	2,330	117	116	132
1960	2,500	126	118	141
1961	2,730	137	123	147
1962	2,870	144	127	151
1963	3,160	159	129	161
1964	3,420	172	135	173
1965	3,670	184	141	187
1966	3,850	193	147	195
1967	4,120	207	150	206
1968	4,390	221	158	222
1969	4,540	228	166	240
1970	4,920	247	179	270
1971	5,940	298	195	294
1972	8,460	425	210	338
1973	9,760	490	232	386
1974	10,200	513	274	478
1975	11,280	567	343	579
1976	12,200	613	395	646
1977	13,200	663	447	706
1978	16,660	837	483	808
1979	21,540	1082	566	967
1980	23,480	1180	653	1154
1981	23,740	1193	730	1277
1982	25,530	1283	776	1376
1983	28,720	1443	815	1480
1984	32,810	1649	852	1590

Source: Nationwide Building Society (1985)

purchase, considerable capital gains could be accumulated through the housing market. This process is well illustrated by examples given by the Anglia, Hastings and Thanet Building Society (1978):

'A junior government clerk, for example, earning £645 in 1958 bought a semi-detached in Walsall for £2,100. This house is now worth £11,000 and with an outstanding balance on the mortgage of £547 his equity stands at £10,453. A milkman who bought a terraced house in Coventry in the same year for £1,325 when he was earning £624 still owns the same house but now worth £8,500, with only £243 owing to the society. A labourer from Wellingborough earning £572 a year in 1964 bought a terraced house for £1,250; it is now worth £4,450, so with his outstanding balance totalling £518, he has an equity of £3,982 if he chose to sell tomorrow. In the same year, a chartered accountant from Potters Bar earning £2,000 a year, bought a semi-detached house for £5,650. This has rocketed in value to £26,000, with £2,720 still to pay off he has an equity in his house of £23,280.'

Such capital gains from the ownership of residential property, together with the expansion of home ownership to more households, have arguably modified the nature and distribution of wealth in Britain (Murie and Forrest 1980). Thus the Diamond Commission on the Distribution of Income and Wealth (Diamond 1976) reported that housing was of increasing importance as a constituent of personal wealth, with the percentage of total personal net wealth accounted for by residential dwellings increasing from 17 per cent in 1960 to 37 per cent in 1975. Existing evidence, therefore, indicates that inflation in house prices has resulted in considerable capital gains accruing to home owners. However any recognition that investors in housing have done rather well over the last two decades or so is excessively general. At issue is not only whether houses, in general, have been a good investment but whether houses, in particular, have been so. Speculating on the stock market may have made many fortunes, but it has also lost many. Are all houses equally good investments or are they like shares and variable in their performance? If variation is discovered then also of interest here is the extent to which this has been the result of wider economic trends.

In this Chapter we examine the evidence, albeit limited, of variation in price gains from one house to another. In so far as this variation is established, and recent surveys do much to confirm this, the Chapter also identifies associations between it and other factors, including variations in labour markets.

Regional house prices and labour markets

In a recent paper Thorns (1982) examines some of the links between the labour and property markets, in the context of the changing economic environment in Britain. In the first part he presents evidence to show the changes which have occurred, and are still occurring, in the labour market. These changes relate particularly to unemployment and thus affect the 'opportunities open to particular sets of individuals' (p. 754). Of particular significance in Thorns' argument is that these changes, as we demonstrated in Chapter three, have had a locational dimension which is apparent in differences in regional levels of both unemployment, and the ratio of unemployment to notified vacancies. For example, he notes that there were 'four times as many unemployed in the Northern region for each vacancy as there are in the South East' (p. 784).

In the second part of his paper Thorns' examines the expansion of home ownership alongside the fact, and significance, of increasing house prices. Drawing upon statistics provided by the Building Societies Association he shows that these increases have not been equal throughout the country, but, rather, indicate large regional differences:

'The South East of England and Greater London, for example, have the most expensive housing and the highest rate of house price inflation. For example, in 1979 house prices rose by 35% in Greater London, and in the rest of the South East by 30%. This compares with a rise of only 18% in the Northern region. Looked at another way, a house in the Northern region would buy only 59% of a house in Greater London and only 63% of a house in the South East region' (Thorns 1982, p. 758).

Thorns goes on to conclude from this evidence that those living in regions which have benefitted from industrial restructuring, and those living in areas which have not, have been respectively rewarded or punished by price changes in the property market:

'These figures indicate the general picture of regional disparities; however, they also mask the true extent of the differences between the prosperous and declining areas when in the latter cases house prices are either static or falling. The results of such marked changes upon owner occupiers in these declining areas is to reinforce their losses sustained by the labour market change. Not only have they lost their job, but also their main private investment, their own house, is also of declining value and virtually unsellable except at a price which would represent a substantial loss to the household' (Thorns 1982, p. 758).

Implied in this argument, therefore, is that in those regions of the country which have experienced rising unemployment, due to industrial restructuring, the resulting fall in personal incomes has lead to reductions in the demand for home ownership. In turn, this has been passed on in the form of reduced house prices so that unemployed home owners are doubly disadvantaged. Thorns continues by drawing attention to the implications of this on the ability of such households to move to a job vacancy in another region:

'The combination of job loss and property value decline has the effect of increasing labour immobilisation, because to move will dramatically increase the costs of the household - either through selling at a loss and thus being in a marginal position to reenter the housing market at a new location, or through being unable to sell or rent the house in the locality from which they have moved and being faced with double housing costs. Because of the regional nature of the declining and expanding sectors of the economy, any moves from declining industrial areas are likely to be ones from low priced housing areas to high priced areas, both in terms of owner occupied and rental housing' (Thorns 1982, p. 758).

In a rejoinder to Thorns, Hamnett (1984) notes that whilst his thesis is 'attractive and compelling', much of its 'elaborate edifice is but a house of cards. Not only is his argument grossly oversimplified and over-generalised, but it is also wholly erroneous' (p. 151). Hamnett presents a number of specific criticisms. The first is that Thorns' evidence of differential regional house price gains does not bear closer scrutiny. Not only has Thorns generalized from data for one year, 1979, to statements about trends over a number of years, but rates of increase over the period 1969-1981 have actually not diverged in the manner suggested. In fact there has been 'a highly lagged pattern of cyclical house price inflation' (p. 152), such that prices in one set of regions have first increased rapidly, with other regions catching up at later dates. As a result, there is no evidence, Hamnett argues, that regional inequalities in house prices have actually increased at all, so that statements about the reinforcement of regional labour market changes by regional housing market changes have dubious foundation in fact.

More recent trends, however, perhaps suggest Thorn's conclusions may well have been correct, even if for the wrong reasons. Table 6.2 shows the average annual rates of house price inflation in each of three periods 1971-1976, 1976-1981, and 1981-1986. The first two time periods demonstrate the normally assumed pattern of differential regional growth. The three areas with the lowest annual rates of growth from 1971 to 1976 – Greater London, the South East and the North West – had the highest rates of growth in the next period. What was lost in those areas in the first five years was therefore largely recovered in the next five years. Rather than the positions being reversed again in the following period, however, Greater London and the South East together with the South West and East Anglia – though not the North West - continued to experience the highest rates of increase. Although the differences in average annual rates of increase have been a few percentage points only, over a decade these have resulted in large absolute differences in capital growth. Thus a house bought in 1976 for £10,000 and located in Greater London would have increased in value, at the average rate of inflation for that region, to £34,300 by 1986. The corresponding 1986 values of houses priced identically in 1976 and located in the South East was £30,000, but located in the West Midlands it was £23,600 and in Northern

Ireland £19,900. Since 1976, therefore, there has been a sustained divergence in levels of both unemployment and house prices with the relatively prosperous area to the south and east of a line joining the Wash to the Bristol Channel becoming relatively more privileged.

Table 6.2 Average Annual Rates of Increase in Regional House Prices (%)

Region	1971-1976	1976-1981	1981-1986
Northern	18.9	12.2	5.3
Yorkshire & Humberside	19.9	14.0	5.6
East Midlands	19.4	12.8	7.5
East Anglia	19.0	14.2	8.3
Greater London	16.0	14.7	11.6
South East (excl. GL)	16.3	14.1	9.2
South West	18.8	14.0	8.1
West Midlands	18.7	13.4	4.7
North West	16.2	14.4	5.3
Wales	18.3	12.6	6.3
Scotland	19.1	12.2	3.5
Northern Ireland	22.6	9.1	5.2
UK	17.7	13.7	7.7

If, as is possible, Hamnett's first criticism has been eroded by more recent trends, his second criticism of Thorn's work remains valid however. This is that in any case the more appropriate measure of labour and housing market changes is not at the regional, but at the intraregional, level. Much of the empirical evidence points to large differences in unemployment and house price levels and trends as between the inner and outer city. As Hamnett points out:

'The regional level may well be too crude and aggregated to reveal the very real discrepancies between house prices in the inner areas and those in the suburban areas and beyond. The same may be true of job loss and unemployment' (p. 160).

119

Implied in this argument, as there was in Thorn's, is that changes in unemployment affect the demand for owner occupied housing. The difference between them, is that Hamnett recognises that the structure of demand and supply may not be homogeneous over a region. Rather, and as we argued in Chapter 2, there may be relatively distinct sub markets demonstrating different trends in supply and demand. Thus within any one region it is possible that there will be white collar and professional groups which have been little hit by unemployment and living within certain housing sub markets, alongside manual groups who have been hit harder and living in other housing sub markets. The occupational and geographical distinctions of course will be blurred but if there is a level of separation this could mean that house prices in one sub market could increase at a faster rate than those in another. A quite different picture might emerge where levels of home ownership were low and unemployment was largely confined to groups who were not home owners. In such circumstances large scale unemployment could exist alongside a buoyant home owner market in which prices were rising rapidly. So it is possible that labour market changes can have a variety of impacts on housing markets. In the case of unemployment its impact would depend, *inter alia*, on the level of overlap between those who were unemployed and those who were home owners.

Limitations of published house price data

What is actually happening to unemployment and house prices within, as opposed to between, regions is an empirical question which has largely gone unanswered, for reasons which perhaps have had less to do with interest and more with data limitations. There is a considerable body of anecdotal evidence about house price levels and trends. With the cessation of the series produced by the Inland Revenue which related to a sample of all sales the currently available published series provide pictures which are partial in some sense. They have been reviewed by the Housing Monitoring Team (1980) who conclude, of the surveys produced by the Royal Institute Chartered Surveyors (RICS) and the Incorporated Society of Valuers and Auctioneers (ISVA), for example, that:

·'The RICS survey would seem to have many faults not least of which is the variations from month to month on the agents reporting prices ... The ISVA survey would appear to be more vigorously organized though it should be noted that only 80 of the ISVA's 7,800 members actually participated in the survey. These agents report from areas designated as 'price points' by the ISVA. Their location is undisclosed' (p. 60).

The remaining series are produced by the Building Societies Association, partly in conjunction with the DOE, and by various individual building societies including the Halifax, Abbey National and the Nationwide. With respect to the type of analysis considered here these series have a number of limitations. Firstly, they rely upon information about houses which have been purchased with the assistance of a building society loan. But as Fleming and Nellis (1981) note: 'From the point of view of measuring house prices this would be of no consequence if there were no difference between the building society sector of the housing market and those served by other sources of finance. There is evidence, however, to suggest that this is not the case' (p. 1114). In fact, the evidence suggests that purchases financed with insurance company and bank loans are of higher priced dwellings than those with building society loans. On the other hand those purchased with the help of local authority loans are generally cheaper (DOE 1977).

Secondly, any unrepresentativeness of these surveys, in terms of price, is compounded by the fact that houses with different characteristics (size, type, location etc.) attract different values. Thus 'changes in average prices over time will reflect changes in the incidence of these (factors) on the houses traded as well as price movements as such' (Fleming and Nellis 1981, p. 1116). As the Housing Monitoring Team show for Dudley in the West Midlands, fluctuations over time in the type of property on the market can be considerable (Housing Monitoring Team 1980). There may be a number of reasons why the mix of housing characteristics might vary from survey to survey. In addition to the fact that the different institutional groups (such as the building societies, banks and local authorities), may be operating in different sectors of the market, within any one institutional group there may also be different market positions. Each building society, bank and insurance company, for example, is an independent body. Within the market in which they operate there are a range of positions to be occupied. Some building societies, for example, may concentrate on certain sorts of property (new as opposed to old) on certain sorts of purchaser (first time or subsequent) and certain sorts of locations (north or south) (Doling and Williams 1983). In addition to this, building societies, for example, may individually or collectively, change their lending policies over time. There may be a swing towards the needs of the first time buyer in which case recorded increases may be as much statements of policy change as about real price changes. Similarly demographic trends may result in changes in the nature of demand so that different sorts of property are being sold.

These 'house characteristic' differences illustrate an important aspect of these surveys which is sometimes overlooked. They record neither the average valuations of a representative sample of houses nor the average of the total value of the housing stock. Rather, they record the average prices of houses for which loans have been approved or taken up. There is no reason to believe that the properties in any one of the surveys, or even all of them together, are necessarily representative of the whole housing stock.

The relevance of this is even more marked when we consider the reported change over time. As Fleming and Nellis (1981) indicate, the reported increases may in part reflect changes in the average size and quality of the housing stock, so that they overrepresent the price increases. Indeed, Hughes (1979) has argued that if general improvements in quality are taken into account house price increases have not, as widely thought, outstripped increases in incomes and prices generally.

Finally, and perhaps most importantly, the series are published at a high level of aggregation. Most of them are disaggregated by region, by house type – detached, terraced and so on, and sometimes by date of construction. However they provide for a level of analysis scarcely finer than that of Thorns. Any evidence of what is happening in different sub markets and/or in different constituent geographical areas of each region is submerged under the weight of information from other sub markets or geographical areas. In the absence of suitable published data the researcher is, therefore, left to grapple with a number of difficulties. Ideally what is required is information about all transactions which can be located within identifiable sub markets in which supply factors are relatively homogeneous.

Variations in local house prices

Given the nature of published data on house prices it is, in retrospect, not surprising that house price increases have commonly been seen as being shared equally amongst home owners. By concentrating empirically on prices at sub regional levels, however, a number of recent studies have begun to throw new light on the issues we have raised. Thorns has also been prominent here. In an earlier paper (Thorns 1981) he took as his starting point the fact that data on house price gains are generally aggregate in nature and that the impression has been given that all home owners have benefitted from the gains. On the basis of an examination of prices in housing sub markets in parts of New Zealand he demonstrates that the data, in fact, 'mask considerable local variation which is related to local market conditions, to the price and location of the property and to the class base of the occupants' (Thorns 1981, p. 206). He goes on to conclude from his analysis of these variations that:

'The largest gains are obtained by those in managerial and professional occupations and in the higher ... income categories. This would seem to indicate that gains from the job and housing markets are in fact quite closely related and to some extent mutually reinforcing. It further shows that owner-occupation

122

has brought greater financial benefits to middle-class home owners than it has to working-class home owners' (p. 213).

Birmingham

The significance of intra regional variations in house price trends has also been suggested using the results of a series of surveys, carried out over the period 1974 to 1981, of recent buyers in four areas of inner Birmingham (Karn, Kemeny and Williams 1985). The four areas - Handsworth, Saltley, Sparkhill and Soho – are dominated by pre-1919 housing, and they constitute the lower strata of the Birmingham housing market. The survey provided information about the purchase price of samples of houses in each area year from 1972 to 1979.

In 1975 the average price of houses sold with a building society mortgage in the West Midlands Region was £10,866, whilst in 1979 it was £18,493, an increase of 14.21 per cent per annum. The corresponding figures for the UK as a whole showed an increase of 16.04 per cent per annum. Over the same period the average annual rates of increase in inner Birmingham were far less than for both the UK and the West Midlands. Using an hedonic price index approach to hold constant the different size and quality variables of the houses sold in each year, the Karn et al data has been recalculated (Doling, Karn and Watt 1984). On this basis Table 6.3 demonstrates that not only did home owners in these four areas receive capital gains which were lower in absolute terms, but also which were lower in relative terms. Even in Saltley where the rise in house prices was most rapid the rate was only about two-thirds of the West Midlands' rate, and indeed diverged from the regional average, much more than the regional average diverged from the national average. Furthermore the extent of intra regional variation can be gauged from the fact that prices in Soho, and therefore rates of increase, actually fell between 1975 and 1979.

This is an important addition to Thorns (1981) since in Birmingham the differences have become greater in both absolute and relative terms. In a financial sense, home owners in these four areas of inner Birmingham could have been better off by investing their capital elsewhere. At this time seven day notice deposit accounts with the London clearing banks were offering rates of interest averaging 11.24 per cent in 1979, and building society ordinary shares offered 8.0 per cent at the start of 1979, 8.75 per cent from 13 July and 10.5 per cent from 22 November. Thus whereas the average home owners in the UK and in the West Midlands region were getting gains in excess of the opportunity cost of their capital, owners in inner Birmingham were not. Indeed over the same period the retail price index increased at an average annual rate of 10.7 per cent so that their assets also failed to keep pace with

123

Table 6.3 Average House Price Increases, Inner Birmingham

Area	Average price (1979) (£)	Average annual % increase (1975-9)
U.K.[a]	19,925	16.04
West Midlands Region[a]	18,493	14.21
Handsworth[b]	8,487	6.94
Saltley[b]	5,030	9.80
Sparkhill[b]	6,710	9.24
Soho[b]	4,530	-1.92

Sources: (a) Building Societies Association

(b) Doling, Karn and Watt (1984)

general price inflation. The disparity between rates of increase in different sub markets also means that home owners in inner Birmingham faced diminishing opportunities for climbing the housing ladder. For those in the areas surveyed the distance between the first and subsequent rungs apparently widened and upward movement necessitated a growth in income and/or savings at a rate commensurate with the rate at which the gap was widening.

These conclusions, however, do not appear consistent with the results of a more recent study of price trends in Birmingham (Moreton and Tate 1986). They used three sources of data: houses acquired by the City of Birmingham for improvement; houses sold by auction; and houses built before 1945 and bought with the help of a loan from the Nationwide Building Society. The authors assumed that these sources would relate to houses at the 'bottom end' of the market though recognising that they might 'disguise sub markets operating in opposite directions' (p. 87). Nevertheless, for the period 1975 to 1984 the authors concluded that the similarity between 'the movement of all the series is too marked to be purely coincidental' and that 'from an investment point of view there is little evidence that [older houses] do not share in the general appreciation within the housing market' (p. 87).

A limitation of the Karn et al study is that it was confined to areas at the very bottom of the housing market so that it is only possible to make general comparisons with other sub markets. In addition the short time period on which the survey was based does not rule out the possibility of different parts of the regional housing market following different cyclical patterns such that lower rates of increase in some years are matched by higher rates in other years with the long term relationship between the strata remaining constant. For the Moreton and Tate study there are questions about the level of aggregation of the data. Research conducted as part of the Coventry study addresses these possible limitations (although it may introduce others) in a number of ways. Firstly, the study areas on which it is based have been selected as being representative of different strata in the housing market. As described in Chapter 2 they range from pre-1919, inner city areas to post war, suburban estates. They thus allow an examination of house price trends across a wide spectrum of the housing market. At the same time each area was selected so that within each one of them the main supply factors were fairly homogeneous. Each contains a large proportion of houses of a certain size and type and built at a certain date. Each is small in area so that location with respect to shops, open space, employment opportunities and so on are fairly constant. The result is that within each area its properties are close substitutes for one other. A second difference in the approach has been to obtain information about house prices over a longer period, namely from 1965 to 1985. The start of this period coincides, with the peak year (1966) for numbers employed in Coventry, whilst the whole period can be viewed as one marked by long term decline in prosperity. It thus provides a basis for examining long term changes in demand and their affects on local housing markets.

Information on house price were obtained for the five years 1965, 1970, 1975, 1980 and 1985 from advertisements under Houses for Sale in the Coventry Evening Telegraph for the first four years, and in The Property Guide for 1985. In this, the present study follows the procedure carried out by the Housing Monitoring Team (1980) which had used advertisements to examine price trends in Dudley over the period 1960 to 1978, and which, although they disaggregated by house type, price and area, found no strong evidence of price divergence over the period as a whole.

The rationale for using advertisements as sources of information about the housing market has been argued by Doling (1978). A criticism of their use is that the prices quoted in advertisements are different from those actually agreed by seller and buyer. The buyer may negotiate the asking price down, or a process of gazumping may bid the price up, for example. But there are also inaccuracies in other data on housing prices. Some building society series, for example that provided by the BSA, record price at both the mortgage approval and the mortgage completion stage, these often being different. In addition, there may be reporting errors such as those where officially recorded prices are underestimates of actual selling prices because they have been dropped to just below a threshold level for stamp duty and compensated for by an informal payment for fixtures and fittings.

Contrasts with national trends

The results of the Coventry exercise are given in Tables 6.4 and 6.5 and Figure 6.1 in which average house prices in each of our study areas at each of the five years are set out alongside corresponding prices of secondhand dwellings in the United Kingdom as a whole. There are thus differences between the national and the local indices. The former are based on a different population at each year with each time period seeing some additional houses built some of which are resold as existing dwellings and some additional houses are brought into the tenure principally from private renting. The Coventry indices, however, are based on a stock of housing which has not been added to by new housing. The effects of these differences on any comparisons are unknown.

The selected survey areas had a variety of average houses prices. Table 6.4 shows that they ranged, in 1965, from £1,681 in Hillfields to £4,056 in Mount Nod. Although three of the areas – Mount Nod, Cheylesmore (semis) and Allesley Park – had averages above the national average they were not greatly above. The remaining six areas had lower averages reflecting the fact that Coventry was not, and is not, an area of high house prices. Over the course of the twenty years since 1965 prices in Coventry have broadly followed national trends. With the exception of the Hillfields and Charterhouse areas, which have displayed unusual features, the remaining areas have followed national trends. With the exception of the Hillfields and Charterhouse areas, which have displayed unusual features, the remaining areas have followed the same pattern of movement found at the national level, and in particular the two marked booms in prices in the 1972-3 period and the 1978-9 period. In itself this is consistent with MacAvinchey and MacLennan's work on regional house prices (MacAvinchey and MacLennan 1982) which demonstrated the significance of national influences on price trends, such as interest rates, over more local ones.

Whilst the general pattern has been the same, however, the rate of increase in Coventry has not kept pace. In the period from 1960 to 1965, prices nationally increased by 40 per cent with those in Coventry increasing by a much lower percentage, generally around 20 per cent, but with the increases in Hillfields and Charterhouse being particularly low. One consequence of this slower rate

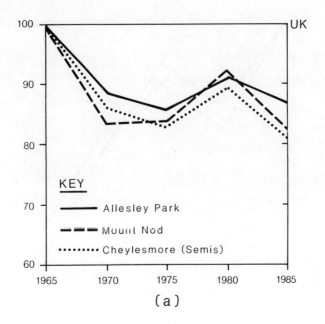

(a)

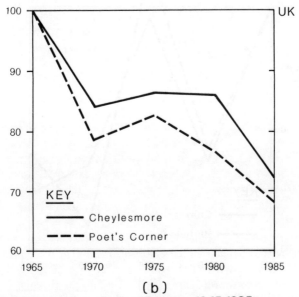

(b)

Figure 6.1 Relative House Price Changes 1965-1985

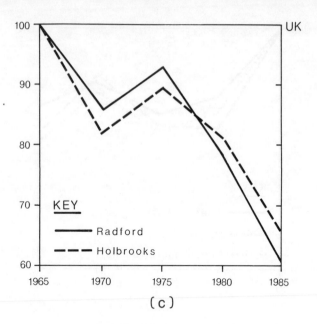

(c)

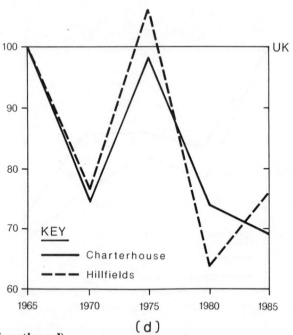

(d)

Figure 6.1 (continued)

Table 6.4 Average House Pices by Study Area (£)

Area	1965	1970	1975	1980	1985
United Kingdom(a)	3576	5010	11880	23085	31224
Mount Nod	4056	4733	11288	24290	29412
Allesley Park	3706	4595	10555	21777	28219
Cheylesmore – semi	3742	4519	10220	21611	26562
Cheylesmore – terrace	3174	3758	9152	17660	20050
Poets Corner	3401	3775	9346	16826	20323
Radford	2898	3340	8606	15203	16686
Holbrooks	2452	2939	7558	12450	13023
Charterhouse	1888	1967	6153	8950	11361
Hillfields	1681	1785	5912	6933	11047

Sources: BSA Compendium of Statistics
             BSA Bulletin
             Coventry House Price Survey

(a)   Prices at mortgage completion stage for existing houses

Table 6.5 Index of Average House Prices by Area, Relative to UK House Prices, (1965 = 100)

Area	1970	1975	1980	1985
Mount Nod	83	84	93	83
Allesley Park	89	86	91	87
Cheylesmore – semi	86	82	89	81
Cheylesmore – terrace	85	87	86	72
Poets Corner	79	83	77	68
Radford	82	89	81	66
Holbrooks	86	93	79	61
Charterhouse	74	98	73	69
Hillfields	76	106	64	75

Source: Coventry House Price Survey

of growth was that by 1970 all the study areas in Coventry had average prices below the national level. In the following period from 1970-75 the Coventry areas held their position with Hillfields and Charterhouse making up the lost ground, but from 1975-80 falling away more markedly. Thus whereas in 1965 the average price over all the study areas in Coventry was 84 per cent of the national average, by 1985 this had fallen to 63 per cent. In addition, whilst house prices increased nationally by 773 per cent, in the Coventry study areas the increases were from 661 per cent down to 431 per cent.

House prices and labour market change

It is pertinent at this point to recall some of the broader changes occurring in Coventry since 1965. Until about the mid 1960s the main indicators of local prosperity had been increasing, and since that time they have been decreasing. Unemployment in Coventry was below the national average until 1967 from which point the underlying trend has been upward with an ever widening disparity. The relatively worsening unemployment picture was also matched by decreases in the total numbers in employment, and the movement of people out of the city as net migration changed from a positive to a negative figure. The indicators thus add up to a picture of a city in which the bubble of post war prosperity burst with the consequence for the housing market of a reduction in consumer demand, which has fed through into house prices.

These figures, then, appear to provide support for Thorns' thesis by indicating the parallels between trends in the labour and housing markets. Specifically, that for those areas of the country like Coventry which experienced restructuring of the local labour market their disadvantageous position in terms of high levels of unemployment, was reinforced by developments in the housing market. The figures here, however, also lead to a conclusion which is at variance with this thesis for reasons which relate to the level of aggregation. It is at least implicit in much of Thorns' 1982 paper that the consequences of industrial restructuring have been experienced most heavily by individuals with certain occupations in certain industrial sectors and for those who are home owners this has been reinforced by their housing position. The point here is that the Coventry data indicate that it is not only those households which have experienced unemployment or some other adverse consequence of the recession who have also experienced relatively lower house prices. All of those home owners in our study areas, and probably all home owners in Coventry, whether or not their incomes have gone up or down, whether or not they have been unemployed, have shared in house price gains which have been lower than those living in other areas.

What this illustrates is a feature of markets in which there are large numbers of buyers and sellers. In such markets price levels are not influenced significantly by individual behaviour but by the behaviour of buyers and sellers *en masse*. Consequently an individual who has not suffered adverse effects of labour market changes, whilst all other home owners in his housing market have, will share their house price losses. Conversely, an individual who experiences loss through labour market change whilst his neighbours do not, will not experience a corresponding house price loss. Thus Thorns has, in fact, analysed only some of the range of possible outcomes in the two markets. This can be illustrated by Table 6.6 where one axis represents the position of the individual in the labour market as either employed or unemployed, and the other the relative price increase in the housing market as a consequence of labour market changes. Thorns' analysis, then, has dealt with situations A and D, where the position of the individual and of the two markets are closely correlated, but not B and C, where they are not.

In relation to Thorns' arguments about the effects of the employment and price changes on mobility these are also more complex than implied. Those in cell D of Table 6.6 may be most disadvantaged, but, in relation to A, those in C and B are also disadvantaged. The former may be unable to change jobs locally, because of a general shortage of jobs, whilst sharing the house price disadvantages of those in D. Those in B are disadvantaged in being presently out of work but at least may have relatively more local job opportunities and house price gains. Those in cell A, however, may be in the most advantageous position having both job opportunities and house price gains.

There is, as we indicated earlier, however, a further level of complexity. It is not necessarily the case that regions are internally homogeneous with respect to supply and demand in their local housing markets. What would seem to be important is the extent to which change in the labour market and particularly unemployment, were experienced by the home owners in an area. If there was little or no overlap then there might be no direct impact on house prices. Indeed this could be the case for the region as a whole if unemployment had mainly been experienced by tenants, or if, within the region, there were some sub markets where there were strong overlaps, and thus marked affects on prices, and other sub markets where there were not strong overlaps, and thus little affect on prices. Thus what may be important is the pattern and extent of overlaps in different sub markets in the region. This suggests a modification of Table 6.6, which explicitly recognises within region variation.

The relative disadvantage of those in the cells of Table 6.7 are then similar to those in the same cells in Table 6.6 except that their position is due not to their regional, but to their sub market, location. Here the adjective similar, rather than the same, has been deliberately chosen because another assumption of Table 6.6 is that unemployment was highest in those regions which already had lowest house prices. This may, in fact, have been the case in the United Kingdom to date but it will not necessarily always be the case. Moreover the modification encapsulated in Table 6.7 make it clearer that it is the house price at the start of any divergences between areas which is also important as a limiting factor in mobility.

Intra-urban variation in prices

It is appropriate at this point to examine further Tables 6.4, 6.5 and Figure 6.1 for evidence of divergence of average prices within Coventry. Continuing to leave aside Hillfields and Charterhouse for the moment, the house price

Table 6.6 Individual and Regional Unemployment and House

		An individual in:	
		Employment	Unemployment
Low regional unemployment –	high price and high price increase	A	B
High regional unemployment –	low price and low price increase	C	D

Table 6.7 Individual and Sub Market Unemployment and House Price Changes

		The individual in:	
		Employment	Unemployment
Low sub market unemployment –	high price increase	A	B
High sub market unemployment –	low price increase	C	D

trajectories for the Coventry study areas have fanned out so that the price distance between them has increased in both absolute and relative terms, with the lower priced areas falling away. Thus in 1965 the average price in the most expensive area, Mount Nod, was 1.65 times larger than the average price in the cheapest area, Holbrooks. By 1985 the difference had grown to 2.26 times.

133

This means that the rungs of the housing ladder in Coventry have not just been getting further apart in absolute terms as might be expected in any case as a result of inflation, but that they are getting further apart in relative terms as well. One consequence is that in order to move from any one rung on the ladder to a higher rung households will have had less assistance from the equity gain in the house they are selling: owner occupation 'far from being a springboard becomes a trap' (Karn et al 1985, p. 106).

In addition to the increasing divergence between areas, there have been marked similarities between some of the areas on each sector. Thus the areas with semi detached housing – Allesley Park, Mount Nod and Cheylesmore – which are the highest priced areas show a broadly similar pattern, which differs from the pattern followed by the areas of terraced housing in Cheylesmore and Poets Corner, for example. This seems to indicate that sub markets have a degree of isolation from one another such that their trajectories can differ. This is not simply a geographical phenomenon – since Cheylesmore terraced and semi behave differently. Equally it is not simply house type because terrace houses in Cheylesmore and Poets Corner differ from those in Radford and Holbrooks. On the other hand their independence is not total. Over the period of the 1970s there is a progression in the trajectories, moving down the market from more highly priced to less highly priced areas. The 1975 peak first emerged in Cheylesmore and Poets Corner, became more pronounced in Radford and Holbrooks, and dramatic in Hillfields and Charterhouse. So, the evidence from Coventry is that intra sub market variations have been less than inter sub market variations. The main pattern which we wish to emphasise here, however, is that prices in the various sub markets have diverged, with prices in more up market areas increasing at a faster rate than those further down market.

In the light of our earlier discussion an obvious question is whether this divergence can be attributed, in full or in part, to labour market changes. Specifically, does this divergence accord with known facts about unemployment and can we point to reasonable hypotheses about the processes which link the two?

The association between houses prices and unemployment is, in some senses perhaps, the easier to establish. In Chapter three it was shown that, against a background of an underlying upward trend in unemployment since the mid 1960s which has affected all parts of Coventry, unemployment has had a differential geographical incidence. In 1971 unemployment was low in five of our study areas – Allesley Park, Mount Nod, Cheylesmore, Poets Corner and Radford – somewhat higher in Holbrooks and highest in Charterhouse and Hillfields. By 1981 this pattern was not dissimilar but the levels of unemployment had changed, so that with the exception of Mount Nod, all areas had higher proportions of their economically active seeking work than there had been in any of the areas in 1971. There is no evidence from the Census of the extent to which this increase in unemployment was experienced by home owners as opposed to tenants, although the likelihood of the unemployed and the home owner forming mutually exclusive groups has been reduced. There is evidence from the household survey, however, that among recent buyers at least the two groups have overlapped and, moreover, that the degree of overlap has been broadly in line with the divergence in price levels between study areas.

Given that the higher the unemployment levels in an area the smaller the percentage increase in house prices, can these be linked causally? At a general, hypothesis-forming, level we can refer back to our discussion earlier in the Chapter about unemployment leading to a reduction in demand. In other words, had the local economy continued to boom after the mid 1960s the demand for home ownership would have continued to expand. There would have been more people with more money some of which they would have been willing to spend on house purchase. Prices in all areas would have risen faster than they actually did, and the sector would have expanded beyond its present level. With a declining local economy, however, there have been fewer people and less money chasing housing. Variation in the geographical incidence of unemployment will have resulted in a greater reduction in the prosperity of some areas than of others, and this in itself may have differentially undermined the demand for housing. More people who, in the absence of rising unemployment, might have been willing to pay higher prices to purchase houses in Holbrooks, for example, in its presence may offer only lower prices or not bid at all. The same may have happened further up market but to a lesser extent as unemployment has had lesser impact numerically. In addition, it can be expected that unemployment will have a different sort of impact, leading to some existing owners to move down market. Those forced to move out as a result of mortgage repayment difficulties may have to sell in a hurry rather than to wait for the right opportunity and right price. Lenders who taken possession of houses are legally required to obtain the best price possible but there is some doubt as to what this means and there is at least some evidence, albeit scanty, that vacant possessed homes do not fetch good prices (Doling, Karn and Stafford, 1985).

Standing alongside the impacts described above it has to be recognised that it is conceivable that there could be sectors in the market which have been isolated or only negligbly affected by changes in the labour market. In very expensive areas, for example, there may have been no discernible slowing in price increases because the sort of people moving in have not been directly affected by unemployment, neither have the existing residents.

So far we have largely disregarded the trajectories of house prices for those two survey areas which constitute part of the bottom end of the housing market in Coventry. Here the patterns have in fact been altogether different. Prices have fluctuated wildly and out of line with other areas. Figure 6.1 shows that over the period 1965-1970 prices in these areas increased far less than in the other survey areas, but in the next five years more than compensated for this. Indeed, in Hillfields house prices had performed quite exceptionally well even in relation to the national average. Then, in the following five years, 1975-1980, they slumped again from being the best to the worst performers of the survey areas, but making something of a recovery over the period 1980-1985.

Hillfields and Charterhouse have experienced higher levels of unemployment than the other six survey areas but whereas the price trajectories in the other six have been variations on a theme, in Hillfields and Charterhouse the theme appears to have been different. What this suggests is that there are influences on house prices other than unemployment and that these other influences may also vary geographically. In this Chapter we now turn to three such influences which provide possible explanations of the unusual price trajectories of Hillfields and Charterhouse, and demonstrate the importance of local supply and demand.

Specifically what is proposed is that there were three factors - planning blight resulting from clearance proposals; improvement grants; and local authority mortgages – which had particular impacts on these two study areas. These impacts were such that they had consequences for house prices, which, in relation to elsewhere, were in some years deflationary and in other years inflationary.

Planning blight Chapter five outlined the changing policy, at both national and local government levels, with regard to the renewal of old residential areas. There is little doubt that in Coventry, as elsewhere, the threat of redevelopment in itself did much to depress housing markets and the lifting of that threat with the turn toward rehabilitation did much to revitalise them (see Dennis 1972; and Shelter 1974). Writing in 1970 of the group of streets in the Hillfields CDA, which were later to become the Winchester Street/Colchester Street GIA, a CDP report sketched out the extent of the uncertainty which had resulted from the Council's plans:

> 'Over the last 20 years the neighbourhood has been continually threatened by redevelopment and at present is blighted for the next 16 years. In 1965 all owners were informed by letter of the pending compulsory purchase of their houses. Several long-standing residents sold their houses to the Council at this time as a result of this threat. Many of the residents remember losing old friends

and neighbours as a result of this false alarm. A number of residents have applied for improvement grants throughout the last 10 years only to be refused by the Council' (CDP 1970, p. 2).

The same report indicated that the first hints of change in the policy of comprehensive redevelopment for this area were not met by an instant boost to confidence.

'Many landlords and owners have said they are unwilling to spend money on the houses, even with grant aid, because they do not know precisely how much longer their houses will be standing. The residents say that the dates have been changed so many times that they are unwilling to believe anyone claiming to have precise information about the future life of their homes' (p. 2).

One consequence of the protracted nature of the programme was that the area suffered from extensive planning blight. A local authority report at the time stated that 'the lack of progress has resulted in vacant sites becoming eyesores and land being used for tipping and fly parking giving the area a depressing and run down appearance. There is no doubt that this decline in the environment has aggravated the multiple social problems experienced in the Inner Areas of the City' (City of Coventry 1972, p. 2). Much the same criticism was levelled from outside the local authority when the CDP (1975, p. 5) noted that 'the council's plans for its comprehensive redevelopment have been cut back or delayed so often over the previous 25 years that for much of the time it has looked like an enormous building site.'

The lifting of the threat of further comprehensive redevelopment was widely welcomed by the residents of areas which had been under threat. Indeed in some areas GIA status had been widely canvassed by local residents prior to any such designation. In some areas, for example the Hartlepool Road/Redcar Road/Stockton Road area, residents associations had been set up and campaigned for area renewal status. Areas of pre-1919 housing adjacent to the Hillfields CDA were themselves under threat of any extension to the existing programme. The 1968 Modified Review Plan, for example, proposed to add to the existing two CDAs in Hillfields and Spon End a further nine CDAs. One of these was the Gulson Road area which bridged our two survey areas of Hillfields and Charterhouse. The blight resulting from uncertainty thus went beyond the designated CDAs themselves. The converse, however, was that in time the lifting of the threat of the bulldozer restored confidence both in the CDAs and beyond. The desire to get out was replaced by a willingness to buy in, and this, we can hypothesize, would have been reflected by increases in prices.

137

Improvement grants Alongside the policy switch from redevelopment to rehabilitation – principally during the period 1970 to 1974 – there was an increase in the number of improvement grants given to private owners by the local authority. Reference back to Table 5.1 shows that over the period 1970 to 1984 Coventry council gave almost 13,000 grants of which 6,589, or just over a half, were given from 1970 to 1974, 20 per cent were given in the second half of that decade, and 30 per cent in the first half of the 1980s.

We saw in Chapter five that in the 1970s many, though certainly not all, of these grants went to areas which were then, or were later to be declared as, urban renewal areas – the GIAs and HAAs. Consequently some of this investment went to the improvement of houses in the Hillfields study area. Of the remaining houses which benefitted from grants these were restricted by statute. Thus under the House Purchase and Housing Act 1959, Improvement or Discretionary grants were restricted to dwellings built before 1945, whereas under the Housing Act 1964 Standard or Intermediate grants were restricted to those built before 1961. These statutes necessarily meant that areas such as Mount Nod and Allesley Park could not benefit from these grants. The Council itself, however, has at various times placed its own and more restrictive limits on grants. In 1973, for example, the Housing subcommittee agreed that no improvement grants would be given to houses built after 1930, and that no improvement grants towards central heating would be given in respect of houses built after 1919.

The position in general terms, then, was that most of the grants were channelled toward housing built before the First World War, some of the grants toward inter war housing, and few toward post war housing. In conjunction with the annual levels of grant allocation shown in Table 5.1 it seems reasonable to suggest that the relative increase on house prices over the period 1970-1975, which was particularly marked in the pre 1919 dwellings of Charterhouse and Hillfields and less so in the inter war dwellings of Holbrooks, Radford, Poets Corner and Cheylesmore, followed from the spatial and temporal variations in the numbers of grants. Public sector investment then has affected the prices house buyers have been willing to pay.

Local authority mortgages Local authorities have long had powers to lend money for house purchase and improvement. Although there have been variations from authority to authority with respect to the types of people and property to whom they lent (see Karn 1976) in general their lending has been 'down market' to those buyers who have found 'access to building societies difficult' (Merrett 1982, p. 100). This is shown by Table 6.8 where, for the country as a whole, the preponderance of lending by local authorities on older property, to first time buyers and large percentage loans is clear.

The annual numbers of loans by local authorities is shown in Table 6.9. Loans by Coventry Council have broadly followed the national pattern although

Table 6.8 Lending by Local Authorities and Building Societies, 1975

(%)

	Building societies	Local authorities
Pre 1919	19.4	62.4
under £4000	0.8	14.9
£4000 – £5999	3.5	15.8
Over £6000	15.1	31.7
Inter war	19.4	19.8
Post war – secondhand	42.7	11.9
New	18.6	5.9
Percentage first time buyers	47	88
Percentage advance	76	90

Source: DOE (1977) Table VII.7.

with the peak period – from 1973 to 1975 – being even more pronounced. In money terms rising from an average of about £2 million per year from 1970 to 1972, to ten times that in 1974. Following that peak, advances declined throughout the remainder of the 1970s, in money terms and in number of approvals and dropped to zero in the 1980s. The picture then is of a large injection of public money into the private housing market in the first half of the 1970s but with smaller injections subsequently.

During the period of peak lending in the first half of the 1970s the terms on which Coventry gave loans were liberal. Firstly the local authority was willing to advance 100 per cent of the valuation of the property. Secondly, the local authority was prepared to give mortgages such that the maximum monthly repayment did not exceed one and a quarter times weekly gross earnings of the head of household. Thirdly, the local authority operated a low start mortgage scheme. This was designed to help those people, particularly young married couples, who because of the size of normal mortgage repayments would otherwise have been unable to buy. The scheme worked such that for the first five years the borrower repaid a nominal £1 per annum of the principal, and paid interest at 1 per cent less than the normal

Table 6.9 Housing Loans by Local Authorities to Private Persons

	No. of loans for private house purchase by local authorities Eng. & Wales [a] (000's)	Advances for house purchase and/or improvement Coventry Council (£)	No. of Coventry Council mortgages for		
			Private house purchase incl. maturity loans	Maturity loans	Council house purchase
1961	62.3	299,366			
1962	53.4	232,322			
1963	57.6	110,952			
1964	77.2				
1965	87.1	3,295,653			
1966	46.2	2,166,924			
1967	56.6	653,030			
1968	38.8	1,220,178			
1969	19.1	392,790			
1970	44.1	1,949,140			
1971	47.2	2,283,890			
1972	45.2	1,270,560			
1973	59.4	14,060,929	3893[b]		
1974	75.4	20,177,330	9682		
1975	102.0	8,879,096	6292		
1976	24.4	6,318,847	6167		
1977	23.5	3,665,097	6083		964
1978	27.3	5,866,920	4157		539
1979	35.5	6,760,298	4597		78
1980	16.4	(-)	0	470	32
1981	4.1	(-)	0	312	688
1982	3.9	(-)	0	407	668
1983	3.1	(-)	0	280	241
1984		(-)	0	289	300

Notes: (a) Calendar years

(b) 4th quarter only

rate for such loans. During the second five years interest was raised to the normal rate. At the end of ten years the loan was treated as a normal annuity mortgage to be repaid over the following twenty years. Being prepared to make 100 per cent advances the scheme was clearly based on the assumption that house prices and incomes would increase. The immediate consequence, however, was that individuals were able to purchase houses which were 25 per cent more expensive than had they taken out a normal repayment mortgage.

If the terms of the mortgages were more generous than could be normally obtained from a building society, the mortgages were also primarily directed at the bottom of the housing market. The maximum loan was restricted to £10,000 and second time buyers were to be given mortgages only in exceptional circumstances. Potential buyers were in any case placed into categories, the definitions of which make it clear that those obtaining local authority loans were marginal to home ownership. These categories were:

(i)   Existing tenants of a local authority or people high on the authority's waiting list for housing; or people displaced by slum clearance or other public authority development whom the council would otherwise have been obliged to rehouse.

(ii)   Applicants who are homeless or threatened with homelessness, or living in conditions that are overcrowded or otherwise detrimental to health.

(iii) ndividual members of self-build groups.

(iv)   Applicants who are wishing to buy older and smaller properties unlikely to attract a mortgage advance from a building society; particularly persons who want to acquire a house with a view to subsequently improving it for their own occupation with the help of a grant under the Housing Act 1969.

(v)   Applicants wishing to buy larger property, in areas where conditions of overcrowding seem liable to develop, with a view to sharing it with other persons, or to converting it into self- contained flats.

(vi)   Staff moving to the area and urgently required in the interests of the efficiency of the public service.

Table 6.10 shows how lending in 1974/5 was dominated by mortgages to categories (i) and (ii). After the peak period of lending, however, the local authority introduced restrictions to limit the availability of mortgages basically to those in the category (i) – existing council tenants and those displaced by slum clearance. Other groups such as key personnel or first time buyers were

Table 6.10 Local Authority Mortgage Lending by Category of Borrower, 1974/75

Category	Amount (£000)	Proportion of total lending (%)
(i)	3593	18.5
(ii)	15419	79.5
(iii)	177	0.9
(iv)	39	0.2
(v)	18	0.1
(vi)	157	0.8
Total	19403	100.0

Source: Memo from Director of Homes and Property Services, 16 July 1975.

excluded. In terms of type and therefore location of property, however, lending continued to be dominated by the older stock. This meant that the impact of local authority mortgage lending – both spatially and temporally – reinforced the impact of grants. They were concentrated at the same time and in the same place.

Conclusion

In Chapter 3 it was argued that in this country the home ownership market had developed recently such that whereas, on the one hand, increasing numbers of home owners had low incomes, on the other hand, the average owners house was apparently increasingly old and requiring increasing amounts of repair. In addition the costs of new production and repair has been increasing. Added to this apparent contradiction the present Chapter has shown that, on average, the market prices of new and secondhand houses had experienced, in the long run, increases which outstripped inflation generally.

On the face of it these various trends appear to confirm our position in Chapter 3 that the impact on the market of low income owners could be ascertained neither from existing studies, because these had been largely in the context of long term prosperity, nor from *a priori* deductions, because the housing market was somehow different from others. By the end of this present Chapter, however, the conclusion may more correctly be that the secret of analysis is to be found in disaggregation and diversity. What has been happening, on average, has disguised what has been happening in different sectors of the market. House price levels and rates of increase have varied greatly from one region to another. The variations between the sub sectors of the market are also significant. What seems to underlie these variations are the supply and demand characteristics prevailing in particular sectors of the market. The analysis of price trends in Coventry suggests that the juxtaposition of low incomes and high prices is not everywhere the same. In some sub markets there appears to be few low income owners. In such areas prices and quality are high. In other sub-markets there are many low income owners including many who have become low income since purchase and houses are of low quality and price increases slower.

This Chapter has also demonstrated, however, that other elements of supply and demand are important in understanding housing market outcomes. If the speculations about the impact of grants and mortgages are sustainable then it follows that massive public investment – over £20 million in 1974 alone – has been the principle difference between sub markets with fluctuating prices and submarkets with rapidly falling prices. Without that investment prices in Hillfields and Charterhouse would not have recovered over the period 1970-1975 but would have kept on falling away. Their distinctive trajectories, then, owe themselves to temporary public support and once this was withdrawn the market turned back to being driven by a level of demand which was falling, relatively, under the impact of unemployment. The speculations also indicate that there are more influences upon house prices than unemployment. High local unemployment will only mean low rates of increase in house prices under certain sets of circumstances.

7 Conclusion

The diversity of home ownership re-examined

The starting point of this book was that home ownership has been traditionally equated with the 'good life'. The usual perception has been that certain benefits accrue to home owners as a direct consequence of home ownership, such that owners got somethings which tenants did not. Owners get capital growth, tenants do not; owners get status, tenants do not; owners get freedom of choice and independence, tenants do not. Attitudinal and behavioural changes are also often thought to follow the transition from renting to ownership. Implicit in these images of the advantages and disadvantages of tenures are also images of the typical physical structures concerned. The stereotype image of the privately rented sector is of a flat or bedsit in a multi-occupied house built in the last century. Set alongside this is the council flat in an inner city tower block with vandalised lifts and grafitti-covered walls: or of a house in a monotonous, and badly maintained, estate. In contrast the home owner has the luxury of a semi-detached, suburban house in good condition, and a garden.

One of the objectives of this book has been to draw together evidence – some previously published and some presented for the first time – which demonstrates something of the diversity of experience within home ownership and therefore the extent to which its image matches reality. This evidence has not allowed the specification of the precise extent of diversity. In many ways the areas of concern are simply under researched. It has not been possible to provide a fine disaggregation by geographical area of mortgage arrears or of house prices, for example. Rather it has been possible to demonstrate, firstly, that diversity of experience does occur and, secondly, that there appear to be patterns of diversity as between parts of the country, and within one city, parts of its housing market. Any image of home ownership as a tenure characterized by homogeneity can be firmly rejected even though the full scope of its heterogeneity has not been established. Any presumption that market provision consistently delivers the benefits normally associated with home ownership can be similarly rejected.

A question which follows from the establishment of a picture of home ownership characterized by heterogeneity is why is there a discordance between this and the traditional image. Putting to one side the issue of the nature and foundation of ideology, our argument has been that there has been a real change, only recently, in the nature of home owners. The benefits of home ownership, as with the benefits of other commodities, have to be paid for and what has happened is that whereas increasing numbers of people have gained access to the tenure, they are not all able to sustain the financial commitment which home ownership entails. There has been, then, a change in the reality of home ownership to which our image of home ownership has not yet been adjusted. The change can be seen as a shift away from a position where all, or the great majority, of home owners had stable or increasing incomes, particularly when inflation ensured that entry costs were decreasing in real terms, and thus the continued payment of housing costs was not generally problematic. For most people entry into the sector was associated with the ongoing receipt of the benefits which they had been purchasing. Where that increasing gap between higher incomes and lower costs did not materialise then the necessary readjustments in a household's pattern of consumption have sometimes resulted in quite different, and adverse, experiences of home ownership.

Historical evidence suggests that there have always been cases of the latter. In recent years, however, their incidence has increased as a result of a number of processes. Two of these are related to incomes. The first is that throughout the course of the present century home ownership has moved down the income scale. Home ownership rates among high income groups in professional and managerial occupations have always been higher than those in lower paid manual jobs. As the sector has increased in size it has done so by recruiting more of those located at all points on the socio-economic spectrum.

The second process is concerned with changes in the economy and, in particular, the job market. We have shown in earlier Chapters that for many individuals there have been changes in the experience of employment. Over the course of the last ten years the level of unemployment has increased rapidly. Insofar as the incidence of unemployment has increased for all sectors or classes of society, home owners have not been immune from its impact. So some home owners, like some tenants, have experienced reductions in their income as a direct consequence of unemployment. This does not mean that all types of home owner have been equally prone to unemployment. The changes in the economy which have brought about unemployment have largely centred on manual workers in the manufacturing sectors. This means, as we described in Chapter three, that unemployment has had a particular impact on certain occupations, certain industries and certain parts of the country. One consequence, however, is that unemployment has been heavily experienced amongst the groups who recently have been more widely recruited into home ownership. So, at the same time as home ownership has been moving down the income and the social class scale, unemployment has been moving up.

There have been other processes, too, which we have noted in earlier Chapters. Marital and relationship breakdown has become increasingly more common so that household income and expenditure flows have been disturbed by changes in household composition. Demographic changes have resulted in greater numbers of elderly home owners many of them living on fairly low incomes.

Insofar as they affect home ownership the combined result of these processes is that more people are entering home ownership with low incomes, or experience a reduction in income once they have entered. So home ownership is no longer exclusively the housing only of higher income groups.

The implications of low income home owners for home ownership, in theory, depends on a number of variables. Principally, these include: whether they were low income when they entered, or after entering; if the latter was this anticipated or accidental and the length of time involved; whether the owner has a mortgage outstanding; and prevailing market prices. Neither can the implications be separated from decisions the individual home owner might make about non-housing areas of expenditure: are economies made on fuel, food and/or holidays?

As far as the home itself is concerned we have drawn together evidence on the implications of low and reduced incomes. For some home owners the decision is to economize on running costs. This leads many to postpone repair and maintenance expenditure with the result that increasing numbers of owner occupied homes are, on the basis of government figures, in an unsatisfactory state of repair. Whilst the average state of repair is apparently deteriorating, however, there is seemingly a polarisation between the many homes which are in good condition – the traditionally well maintained owner occupied housing – and the many which are not. Not all of those in the latter group are there because their owners have fallen on hard times. Some will be in that condition because the people buying them had incomes so low that that was all they (or their mortgagee) deemed they could afford. With no subsequent upturn in their fortunes they have continued to live in poorly maintained housing. Some owners are also in poorly maintained housing out of choice rather than as a result of poverty.

There is an extent to which such behaviour is not only an income issue but is reinforced by the investment implications of home ownership. Whereas it is often assumed that home owners will seek to maintain the physical quality of their homes because this will enhance its market value, the reality is that the market does not always have this effect. It may, rather, be financially advantageous to let the property deteriorate, with this often seeming to be the case at the lower end of the market. Thus, in some areas at least, the market value of an improved house may be less than the sum of the market value of an unimproved house and the cost of carrying out improvements. Consequently households which, by virtue of their incomes, move into an area of predominantly unimproved or run down housing may have no investment incentive to upgrade them. Neither may there be any investment incentive to maintain the property at even its present state of repair. If, subsequently, the household does wish to increase the quality of its housing – perhaps because its income has increased – it might be better off financially moving to another house which has already been improved or repaired. This means that the spontaneous upgrading of areas of low quality housing will be limited in numbers. It is unclear why there should be this relationship between the market values of improved and unimproved housing, but it may be a market response to the demand for low quality housing. In other words this should perhaps not to be looked at as, necessarily, an aberration or failure of the market, but as the consequence of the nature of demand. Decreasing housing quality may, then, be thought of as the result of increasing numbers of low income owners who have a low demand for housing. In this sense it may be a reflection of inequality of income amongst consumers in this market.

There are, however, other aspects of market incentives for repair and improvement which derive not from the nature of demand but from the nature of the product. Specifically, the benefits from expenditure on improvements and repairs may be differently experienced. There is evidence that the benefits of improvements are enjoyed primarily by the individual home owner, but that he shares the benefits of his expenditure on repairs with his neighbours. The market value of the individual house is then heavily constrained by the quality of the nearby houses, with disrepair being one of the consequences.

The trends in disrepair and condition generally cannot, however, be understood only in terms of individual budgetary decisions in the context of market processes and constraints. Government policy has been important too. There is now a long history of urban renewal in the form of redevelopment and of rehabilitation. Many homes which have been unfit, lacking amenities or in a poor state of repair have been demolished or received some form of grant-aided expenditure. This has been particularly directed toward housing which has had inner city locations, was built before 1919 and had poorer tenants and owners. To an extent this has countered the trends arising from increasing numbers of low income owners.

Whilst for many home owners changing income levels force a reappraisal of the running costs of ownership, this may be done separately, or in conjunction with a reassessment of the entry costs. The nature of house purchase, in practice, frequently results in buyers making long term financial commitments in the form of mortgage repayments. Where incomes are low and/or loan-income ratios high - sometimes because income has fallen – maintaining the mortgage may be difficult. The trend over the course of the 1980s has seen a year by year growth in the numbers of owners who fail to meet their financial commitments with the result, for some of them, that they lose their homes. Sometimes this means moving down market and sometimes becoming a tenant. In the short term it may mean lodging with friends or relatives, or even homelessness. The increasing numbers of home owners so affected belie the notion that home ownership is necessarily about the ladder to success. Or that it, unlike renting, provides security of tenure.

If financial hardship amongst individual home owners has resulted in them experiencing difficulties in meeting entry and/or running costs, there have been wider effects in the form of price changes. Seemingly as home ownership has expanded there has been an increasing divergence in market prices as between prosperous regions and poor regions, and within regions between its prosperous and poor parts.

Nationally, this has manifested itself as a gap between prices in the south and south east of the country, and in the midlands and north, which has been increasing in size over an extended period of time. Within the Coventry housing market price gaps between market strata have been growing since at least the mid 1960s. One explanation seems to be that low income home owners, particularly evident in levels of unemployment, have dampened demand in some regions and sub-markets relative to others. The gaps are then products of the changing (lower income) nature of home owners combined with economic restructuring. On this view, there is a link between the spheres of production and consumption such that those who are disadvantaged in the former, especially by virtue of unemployment, are also disadvantaged in the latter, by virtue of relative losses in the value of their homes.

It is clear, however, that this analysis is oversimplistic. Whether or not there is increasing price divergence, and if there is, whether this can be related to unemployment is dependent on a large number of supply and demand factors. Where there was no, or little, overlap between the body of home owners and the body of the unemployed there might be no dampening of demand. Alternatively if an unemployed home owner lived in a sub market in which other home owners were not unemployed then his disadvantage in the sphere of production might not be passed on to the sphere of consumption. The corollary is that an employed home-owner in a sub market of predominantly unemployed owners would be advantaged in the sphere production but

148

disadvantaged in the sphere of consumption. One thing which this illustrates is that in the housing sphere one owner's fortune is dependent to a large extent, on the fortunes of his neighbours. There is also in this, a link with our earlier conclusions about the investment incentives of improvement and repair. The rewards to be gained from the housing market derive more from the features of the sub market than from the house itself. Analysis of the Coventry price trajectories also indicates that there are other supply and demand factors which may be important. Over the last twenty years the relative prices of housing at the bottom of the market have oscillated widely apparently as a result of changes in credit availability and public subsidy. One of the consequences, therefore, is that what has proved, over the years, to be a good investment for many, may have been for some only mediocre and for others quite poor. It cannot be assumed that all home owners will get the same rate of capital appreciation.

The nature and meaning of home ownership

The increasing diversity within home ownership also means that the nature and meaning of home ownership is changing. Home ownership can no longer be viewed as the exclusive preserve of the 'haves' who are in an advantageous position in contrast to the 'have-nots' who rent their homes. Home ownership is no longer exclusively about high quality housing which confers benefits on owners. Rather home ownership in terms of its meaning and benefits is becoming more diffuse. Forrest and Murie (1983, p. 465) make much the same point when they argue that:

> 'As home ownership expands its image as a positional, high status good is progressively undermined. Our image of home ownership as a tenure which confers status and relative affluence derives from a time when those positional advantages were only enjoyed by a minority'.

One consequence of this shift is that there are tranches of home ownership which bear stronger resemblances to the traditional image of the rental tenures than they do to their own tenure. If buyers can afford so little relative to the general level of prices in the home ownership market, then they will have few choices about where to live. If they are competing at the bottom of the market, or if they are further up the market but unable to meet maintenance costs, then their homes may be in poor condition. If they have purchased in certain sections of the market any capital invested might be appreciating at a slower rate than if it had been invested in a building society account, and consequently they are not benefitting from capital growth. If they are unable to meet their mortgage repayments in full, then the body from whom they have borrowed may take them to court to obtain possession of the property. So, if some home owners have few choices about the location and nature of their home, the home is in poor physical condition, it provides no real capital gain and they have little security of tenure there may be little which distinguishes them from the stereotype of a tenant. Indeed if they end up with less capital than they started with, then they might be said to be in an inferior position to the tenant.

If there is a greater heterogeneity within home ownership this has implications also, for the commonly-drawn association between tenure and class. In the past home ownership has been seen as the preserve of those, 'by and large, relatively advantaged in terms of class background' (Forrest and Murie 1983, p. 465). Moreover, because the majority of working class people were tenants, while 'the overwhelming proportion of the upper classes own or are buying their houses' (George and Wilding 1984, p. 93), the conclusion was often reached that 'the association between social class and housing tenure is very strong' (George and Wilding 1984, p. 93).

Whilst tenure reflected class divisions so that the one could be used as a proxy measure for the other, as home ownership moved down market to incorporate more lower income and working class groups, class divisions have become absorbed within home ownership. A process of internalization has taken place such that tenure itself may no longer be relevant to, or associated with, class divisions. There may be nothing to distinguish the poor tenant from the poor owner. Both may be deprived in their command over society's scarce resources with their housing circumstances neither adding to, nor detracting from, that deprivation. The boundary between the 'haves' and the 'have-nots' no longer coincides with the boundary between tenures. Rather the distinction, now, may be between those with higher incomes living in owner occupied homes situated in the middle and upper ranges of the housing market, and those living either in the lower ranges of the owner occupied housing market or in tenanted property. The divisions of course, will, in reality, be blurred. Some higher income groups continue to rent, for example. Such blurring has always been there, but what is important is that the division between home owners and tenants has diverged from the division between the 'haves' and the 'have-nots'.

The changing nature of home ownership does not mean, however, that many home owners do not benefit from their home. House price increases in 1986 and 1987, most marked in London and the South East, have again emphasised the good investment record of some dwellings. Many home owners have thus seen a return on their money which has outstripped the potential returns on similar risk, or indeed some higher risk, investments. Equally many home owners have continued to benefit from those attributes – independence, status, choice, high quality - traditionally associated with their tenure. It is not,

150

therefore, that the nature and meaning of home ownership has changed for every individual. For many their individual and immediate experiences are consistent with the stereotype picture of home ownership. Home ownership of the traditional type with the traditional benefits continues, but there is also a growing part of the tenure which does not share many of those benefits. There is, as we suggested in Chapter one, firm evidence of individuals experiencing 'bad' and 'good' home ownership.

The limits to home ownership

One response to the evidence of the financial difficulties experienced by many home owners is to argue that limits of the sector are being reached. That is that the sector has expanded down the income scale to a point where many people are in fact marginal to the tenure. There is a broad band of people all of whom, in the present environment, may be close to the point where small disturbances to incomes or expenditures affect their ability and willingness to continue to meet existing housing costs. For some these disturbances may not occur. Of those for whom they do the disturbances may be small, short-term or their impact nullified by the adaptations taken by the household. For some, however, the outcome will be experienced in the failure to meet some or all of their housing costs. As we have shown this means that some home owners experience a decline in the level of housing services they enjoy, and in the rate of capital appreciation. For some it also means that their status as home owners is threatened and they revert to one of the rental sectors.

All other things being equal, as this band of home owners 'at risk' increases then we can expect there to be more casualties. Structural changes – say in the labour market or in the distribution of income and wealth – will result in a widening or a narrowing of this band. Thus groups who may be at risk under one set of initial conditions, will not be under other sets.

Another response is the consideration of how the structural conditions might be changed, perhaps through government action, and in particular through government action with respect to housing subsidies. In Chapter 3 it was shown that the principal subsidy to home owners - mortgage interest relief – provided more help to those on higher incomes. Thus most subsidy is paid by those who pay the highest marginal rate of income tax and have mortgages of £30,000 or over. There is a geographical expression to this. In the Coventry study areas the average subsidy received in the up market area of Mount Nod was almost twice that received in the down market area of Hillfields.

Insofar as home owners take on mortgage commitments which at the time they are able and willing to meet from their incomes, the subsidy they receive also reflects that income. Where there are subsequent changes in income these can, if they alter the marginal rate of tax, lead to change in the amount of subsidy received. An important characteristic of this is that if income falls the amount of subsidy will remain static or decrease: it cannot increase. This means that not only do lower income buyers receive less assistance in the form of MIRAS than do higher income buyers, but if their income falls they also will not receive any compensating assistance through MIRAS. As a subsidy therefore MIRAS is one which, like the decision to purchase in the first place, is in practice based on an assumption of a continued ability to meet the financial commitment of purchase. It is not a 'safety net' subsidy and its appropriateness in ameliorating many of the situations with which we have been concerned is clearly questionable.

Although MIRAS is not a safety net subsidy, however, there are subsidies available to some owner occupiers which do in part, fulfill this function. Firstly there are a range of benefits – unemployment benefit, child benefit, family income supplement and so on – to which home owners and tenants alike may be eligible. There are two such benefits which contain specific housing elements: supplementary benefit and housing benefit. The rules of eligibility, however, restrict the numbers of recipients. Housing benefit is means tested whilst supplementary benefit is restricted to those with under £3,000 capital and without a full time job.

It could be argued that if home ownership is to expand further this can only be achieved with 'reasonable' accommodation and conditions of security of tenure if lower income groups receive greater subsidies. What would be required is, failing a major and more general redistribution of income and wealth, a subsidy system which does not expend most resources on those groups who are not marginal to home ownership. If the object is to expand the sector it seems likely that, given its perceived benefits, middle and upper income groups may not require financial inducements to do so. To that extent MIRAS is poorly targetted. Targetting marginal or low income buyers would require a system which had at least some of the characteristics of supplementary benefit and housing benefit, namely being means tested and housing cost tested.

Housing markets and equality

In Chapter one we argued that the popular and traditional perception of home ownership concurred with emergent political views, associated with the New Right, that competitive markets were generally preferential to state provision. Thus recent political rhetoric was summarized as an argument that there was an inequality in the benefits enjoyed by home owners and tenants from their respective tenures. In particular, home owners were inevitably gainers merely because they owned their own homes. The reader is reminded of the quotation, in Chapter one, by the Secretary of State for the Environment who asserted that tenure formed the 'greatest division' in our society as between the haves and the have nots. This view appears to stand in contrast with another, also widely held, that housing has been one of the few successes of policies in Britain aimed at achieving equality. In his influential book on the achievement of equality through the welfare state Le Grand (1982) concluded that in reality public spending has been distributed in a way which broadly favours the higher social groups. In essence, such spending has tended not to advantage those groups whom it was putatively aimed to favour. This has not been exclusively so, though the exceptions are limited. Le Grand, indeed, limits the 'established exceptions in developed countries' to 'public housing, rent rebates and allowances, the US Medical System and means-tested elements in the education sector, all programmes that are confined by policy decision to people on low incomes' (Le Grand 1982, p. 128). According to Le Grand, then, in Britain council housing together with its means tested rent rebates (now housing benefit) has been one of the very few welfare measures which have proved effective in redistributing resources in favour of poorer groups.

This conclusion is consistent with the long-established claim that the achievement of council housing in Britain has been to break the link between housing and income. The rules of access have been such that who gets what housing is determined not by who can pay most but by whose need is considered greatest. It is now clear that the correlation with need is far from perfect. Henderson and Karn (1987), for example, have shown the extent to which the 'undeserving poor' in general and ethnic minority groups in particular have been relatively disadvantaged in the council house allocation process. Nevertheless, outcomes consistent with an assessment of needs have been far greater with public than with private housing.

There seem to be two arguments, therefore. The first that home owners receive more benefits from their home than do tenants. The second that in public housing the outcomes are more equal than they would be with a market allocation. Given these two arguments under what circumstances would they justify a transfer from public to private provision? In particular, would the transfer result in individuals necessarily being better off? This would only be the case, invariably where all home owners are better off than all tenants. Any transfer from renting to owning would cause an automatic gain in individual welfare. But where the benefits of owning and renting overlap in the sense that some owners are worse off than some tenants, the benefits of becoming an owner are not automatic. Seen from the point of view of the individual, therefore, it is an empirical question as to whether home ownership is better than renting at a particular point in time.

On the basis of the evidence which we have examined home ownership has not eliminated inequality in housing consumption, nor closed the 'divide'. For some home ownership has proved to be a new form of inequality. For them

153

their initial state of inequality, by virtue of not being a home owner, has not been improved by becoming one. Their extent and type of inequality has remained as it was. Conceivably for some of those whose incomes have fallen after they entered home ownership their objective situation has worsened. There is a real sense in which inequalities within home ownership now reflect wider societal inequalities in other spheres, notably income and wealth.

Any apparent inconsistency in the arguments, however, might be resolved by a different interpretation of equality to that implied above. Here the term has been used in the sense of 'prospect regarding' equality (see Rae 1981, p. 62) to mean that government is increasing the opportunities for people to become home owners and to share the benefits of that position. As we have shown, however, this wider sharing of the benefits has been limited. This has been because home ownership policies have not sufficiently addressed the income distribution side of the equation. Everyone may be given equal opportunities to enjoy the benefits of home ownership but not everyone has the income to do so. The equality which is being pursued is thus of the 'means regarding' type, in which all do not share because market prices ration out the prospects for lower income households. The freedom of choice and the crossing of the divide between the haves and the have nots, espoused by the New Right, is of the means regarding variety, masquerading often under the guise of the prospect regarding variety.

In making these comments, however, we should be wary of arriving at simple generalizations about what markets and what state provision can do. Although it is common to talk about the distinction between the public and private sectors, and between state provision and market provision the distinctions are actually not that clear. The reality is that markets do not exist in a vacuum, but operate within a framework of institutional contingencies which include legislative regulation, linkages with other markets (and their institutional frameworks), market actors and the distribution of resources amongst them. These institutional arrangements differ as between different markets, so that 'what is shared by all markets is little more than the fact that something is marketed in them' (Hindess 1987, p. 150). This means that it is not possible to generalize, fully, about the market or about market outcomes: 'the point is that the consequences of market allocation (of toothbrushes, housing or old-age pensions) cannot be determined independently of what those insitutional conditions are' (Hindess 1987, p. 150). The distinctions, moreover, are not only between the markets in toothbrushes, housing, old-age pensions and so on but will be spatially and temporally specific.

We have seen in our research that the institutional framework of the Coventry housing market in the second half of the 1970s included local authority mortgage lending, grants for repairs and improvements and rehabilitation policies, and a labour market buoyant relative to the 1980s. The result, as we have posited, was that these set of phenomena boosted prices at the lower end of the Coventry housing market relative both to other parts of Coventry's market and to the national trends. Similarly the changed circumstances of the institutional framework in the first half of the 1980s has resulted in a different set of price movements. Local market conditions can differ at any one point in time so that market outcomes in different parts of the country will be different. This point is argued by Dickens et al. (1985). Whilst seeing capitalism as an 'overarching social structure and an international economic system' they nevertheless put the proposition that 'what are identified as basic structural mechanisms actually produce widely variable outcomes in different times and at different places' (p. 1). The general point, then, is that because certain outcomes are apparent in one place at one point in time we cannot assume that they will be similar in other places and at other times. Indeed our emphasis on diversity has to an extent been based on this very premise.

Bibliography

Anglia, Hastings and Thanet Building Society (1978) *Survey of Mortgage Advances by the Anglia, Hastings and Thanet Building Societies over the Past Twenty Years*, Anglia, Hastings and Thanet Building Society.

Ashley, P. (1983) *The Money Problems of the Poor: A Literature Review*, SSRC/DHSS Studies in Deprivation and Disadvantage 11, Heinemann, London.

Balchin, P. (1985) *Housing Policy: An Introduction*, Croom Helm, London.

Ball, M. (1983) *Housing Policy and Economic Power*, Methuen, London.

Boleat, M. (1984) 'Modest downturn in arrears cases at end of 1983', *Building Societies' Gazette*, No. 1407, pp. 414-416.

Bosanquet, N. (1983) *After the New Right*, Heinemann, London.

Bowley, M. (1945) *Housing and the State 1919-1945*, Allen and Unwin, London.

Building Societies Association (1985) *Mortgage Repayment Difficulties*, Report under the chairmanship of Mr. Mark Boleat, BSA, London.

Building Societies Association (1986) *BSA Bulletin No. 48*, BSA, London.

Burnett, J. (1978) *A Social History of Housing 1815-1970*, David and Charles, Newton Abbot.

CIPFA (1982) *Finance and General Statistics 1982-1983*, Chartered Institute of Public Finance Accountants, London.

City of Coventry (1961) *Hillfields CDA Redevelopment Policy: Analysis of the Problems of Residential Redevelopment*, City of Coventry, Coventry.

City of Coventry (1963) *First Quinquennial Review of the Development Plan: Work in Coventry*, Report No. DPR 33, City of Coventry, Coventry.

City of Coventry (1966) *First Review of Development Plan: People and Housing*, City of Coventry, Coventry.

City of Coventry (1972) *Comprehensive Development Areas: Report on Future Programming for Clearance*, City of Coventry, Coventry.

City of Coventry (1984) *Information Digest*, Prepared by Environmental Health Services Department, City of Coventry, Coventry.

Conservative Party (1987) *The next moves forward: the Conservative manifesto*, Conservative Central Office, London.

Coventry Community Development Project (1970) *CDP Final Report: Part 1: Coventry and Hillfields: Prosperity and the Persistence of Inequality*, CDP, London.

Coventry Community Development Project (1975) *CDP Final Report: Part 2: Background Working Papers*, CDP, London.

Crossman, R. (1970) 'Introduction', *Sent to Coventry*, (Hodgkinson, G.), Robert Maxwell and Co., London.

Culley, L. and Downey, P. (1986) *Mortgage Arrears: Owner Occupiers at Risk*, Association of Metropolitan Authorities, London.

Davis, O. (1960) 'A pure theory of urban renewal', *Land Economics*, pp. 220-226.

Dennis, N. (1972) *People and Planning*, Faber and Faber, London.

Department of Health and Social Security (1983) *Social Security Statistics 1983*, HMSO, London.

Department of Health and Social Security (1986) *Social Security Statistics 1986*, HMSO, London.

Department of Health and Social Security (1984) *For Richer for Poorer? DHSS Cohort Study of Unemployed Men*, Research Report No. 11, HMSO, London.

Department of the Environment (1977) *Housing Policy Technical Volume Part II*, HMSO, London.

Department of the Environment (1979) *National Dwelling and Household Survey*, HMSO, London.

Department of the Environment (1982) *English House Condition Survey 1981 Part 1 Report of the Physical Condition Survey*, HMSO, London.

Department of the Environment (1983) *English House Condition Survey 1981 Part 2 Report of the Social Survey*, HMSO, London.

Department of the Environment (1985) *Analysis of Arrears Return of Local Authority Housing Activity (P3 Part F) Outstanding loan debt and mortgage arrears, repossessions and vesting: England 1983/84*, Mimeo, DOE, London.

Diamond (1977) *Royal Commission on the Distribution of Income and Wealth*, HMSO, London, Cmnd. 6990.

Dickens, P., Duncan, S., Goodwin, M. and Gray, F. (1985) *Housing States and Localities*, Methuen, London.

Doling, J. (1978) *The Identification of the Determinants of House Prices*, Environmental Modelling and Survey Unit, University of Birmingham, Birmingham.

Doling, J. (1983) *Who are the Low Income Owner Occupiers? An Empirical Study of Birmingham*, Working Paper 89, CURS, University of Birmingham, Birmingham.

Doling, J. (1986) 'Owner occupation, house condition and government subsidies', *Low Cost Home Ownership*, (Booth, P. and Crook, eds.), Gower, Aldershot, Hants.

Doling, J., Karn, V. and Stafford, B. (1984) *A Study of Mortgage Possession Actions in Coventry County Court*, Working Paper No. 96, CURS, University of Birmingham, Birmingham.

Doling, J., Karn, V. and Stafford, B. (1985) *Behind with the Mortgage*, NCC, London.

Doling, J., Karn, V. and Stafford, B. (1986) 'The impact of unemployment on home ownership', *Housing Studies*, Vol. 1, No. 1, pp.49-60.

Doling, J., Karn, V. and Watt, P. (1984) *The Reform of Housing Finance: Its Impact on Low Income Owner Occupation*, Mimeo, CURS, University of Birmingham, Birmingham.

Doling, J. and Stafford, B. (1987) 'Regional variations in mortgage arrears', *Area*, Vol. 19, pp. 103-109.

Doling J. and Thomas, A. (1982) 'Disrepair in the national housing stock', *Town Planning Review*, Vol. 53, No. 3, pp. 241-256.

Doling, J. and Williams, P. (1983) 'Building societies and the local housing market', *Environment and Planning A*, Vol. 15, pp. 663-673.

Donnison, D. (1979) 'Housing the poorest people', *Housing Review*, March/April, pp. 48-49.

Duncan, S. and Kirby, K. (1983) *Preventing Rent Arrears*, HMSO, London.

Farthing, S. (1975) 'Housing in Great Britain', in *Reviews of United Kingdom Statistical Sources, Vol. III*, (Maunder, W., ed.), Heinemann, London.

Farmer, M. and Barrell, R. (1981) 'Entrepreneurship and government policy: The case of the housing market', *Journal of Public Policy*, Vol. 1, pp. 307-332.

Finnis, N. (1978) 'Mortgage arrears: tomorrow's problems', *Roof*, January, pp. 10-11.

Fleming, M. and Nellis, J. (1981) 'The interpretation of house price statistics for the United Kingdom', *Environment and Planning A*, Vol. 13, pp. 1109-24.

Ford, J. (1984) *Mortgage Arrears*, Mimeo, Department of Social Sciences, Loughborough University of Technology, Loughborough.

Ford, J. (1986) 'Home owners at risk', *Roof*, July/August, p. 8.

Ford, J. and Took, L. (1986) *Owner Occupation and Mortgage Arrears*, Mimeo, Department of Social Sciences, Loughborough University of Technology, Loughborough.

Forrest, R. and Murie, A. (1983) 'Residualization and council housing: aspects of the changing social relations of housing tenure', *Journal of Social Policy*, Vol. 12, pp. 453-68.

Gee, D. (1975) *Slum Clearance*, Shelter, London.

George, V. and Wilding, P. (1976) *Ideology and Social Welfare*, Routledge and Kegan Paul, London.

Gibson, M. and Langstaff, M. (1982) *An Introduction to Urban Renewal*, Hutchinson, London.

Gow, H. (1985) 'Maintenance and modernisation – A discipline in search of a philosophy?', *Housing Review*, November/December, pp. 187-188.

Griffiths, D. and Holmes, C. (1984) 'To Buy or Not to Buy ... is that the Question?' *Marxism Today*, May, pp. 8-13.

Greater London Council, (1981) *The Greater London House Condition Survey*, GLC, London.

Hamnett, C. and Williams, P. (1979) *Gentrification in London 1961-1971: an empirical and theoretical analysis of social change*, Research Memorandum 71, CURS, University of Birmingham, Birmingham.

Hamnett, C. (1984) 'The post-war restructuring of the British housing and labour markets: A critical comment on Thorns', *Environment and Planning A*, Vol. 16, pp. 147-161.

Hansard, 17 June 1979.

Hansard, 19 February 1986.

Harloe, M. (1985) *Private Rented Housing in the United States and Europe*, Croom Helm, London.

Harrison, A. (1979) 'The valuation gap: A danger signal', *CES Review*, December, pp. 101-103.

Healey, M. and Clark, D. (1984) 'Industrial decline and government response in the West Midlands: the case of Coventry', *Regional Studies*, Vol. 18, No. 4, pp. 303-318.

Henderson, J. and Karn, V. (1987) *Race, Class and State Housing: Inequality and the Allocation of Public Housing in Britain*, Gower, Aldershot, Hants.

Hindess, B. (1987) *Freedom, Equality and the Market: Arguments on Social Policy*, Tavistock Publications, London.

Hodgkinson, G. (1970) *Sent to Coventry*, Robert Maxwell and Co., London.

Housing Act 1957, Chapter 56, HMSO, London.

Housing Monitoring Team (1980) *House Price Analysis: Monitoring the Private Housing Market*, CURS Research Memorandum 83, University of Birmingham, Birmingham.

Hughes, G. (1979) 'Housing income and subsidies', *Fiscal Studies*, Vol. 1, pp. 20-28.

Ingram, G. and Oron, Y. (1977) 'The production of housing services from existing dwelling units', *Residential Location and Urban Housing Markets*, (Ingram, G., ed.), Ballinger, Cambridge.

160

IDS (1971) 'New agreements at Chrysler's Coventry plants', *IDS Report 123*, pp. 3-4.

Jacobs, S. (1981) 'The sale of council houses: does it matter?', *Critical Social Policy*, Vol. 1, No. 2, pp. 35-53.

Johnson, C. (1986) 'Fiscal privilege for housing – can it ever be reformed?', *Supplement to Inquiry into British Housing*, National Federation of Housing Associations, London.

Johnson, J., Salt, J., and Wood, P. (1973) *Housing and the Migration of Labour in England and Wales*, Saxon House, Farnborough, Hants.

Karn, V. (1976) *Priorities for Local Authority Mortgage Lending: A Case Study of Birmingham*, CURS Research Memorandum 52, University of Birmingham, Birmingham.

Karn, V. (1979) 'Pity the poor home owners', *Roof*, January, pp. 10-14.

Karn, V., Kemeny, J. and Williams, P. (1985) *Home Ownership in the Inner City: Salvation or Despair*, Gower, Aldershot, Hants.

Kemeny, J. and Thomas, A. (1984) 'Capital leakage from owner occupied housing', *Policy and Politics*, Vol. 12, No. 1, pp. 13-30.

Kemp, P. (1987) 'Some aspects of housing consumption in late nineteenth century England and Wales', *Housing Studies*, Vol. 2, No. 1, pp. 3-16.

Kilroy, B. (1979) 'Housing finance: why so privileged?', *Lloyds Bank Review*, No. 133, July, pp. 37-52.

Kirwan, R and Martin, D. (1982) *The Economics of Urban Residential Renewal and Improvement*, CES Working Paper 77, London.

Lancaster, (1985) 'Housing the workers: a survey of popular housing in modern Coventry', *Local History Bulletin*, Issue 6, pp. 3-12.

Land, H. (1983) 'Poverty and gender: the distribution of resources within the family', *The Structure of Disadvantage*, SSRC/DHSS Studies in Deprivation and Disadvantage 12, (Brown, M., ed.), Heinemann, London, pp. 49-71.

Le Grand, J. (1982) *Strategy of Equality*, Allen and Unwin, Hemel Hempstead.

Lord Chancellors Department (1982) *Judicial Statistics England and Wales for the year 1981*, HMSO, London.

Lord Chancellors Department (1983) *Judicial Statistics England and Wales for the year 1982*, HMSO, London.

Luce, R. and Raiffa, H. (1957) *Games and Decisions: Introduction and Critical Survey*, John Wiley, New York.

Maclennan, D. (1982) *Housing Economics: An Applied Approach*, Longman, London.

Macgregor, A. (1977) 'Intra-urban variations in unemployment duration: a case study', *Urban Studies*, Vol. 14, No. 3, pp. 303-314.

Mallier, A. and Rosser, M. (1982) *Industrial Decline in Perspective - The Coventry Car Industry*, Staff Seminar Discussion Paper No. 47, Department of Economics, Lanchester Polytechnic, Coventry.

161

Marcuse, P. (1972) *The Financial Attributes of Home Ownership for Low and Moderate Income Families*, Urban Institute Working Paper 209-1-2, Washington, D.C.

Marlow, D. (1979) *The Socio-Economic Impact of a GIA on its Residents*, B.A. Dissertation, Department of Urban and Regional Planning, Lanchester Polytechnic, Coventry.

Matthews, R. (1983) 'Conditions suspicions', *Roof*, March/April, pp. 22-24.

McAvinchey, I. and Maclennan, D. (1982) 'A regional comparison of house price inflation rates in Britain, 1967-76', *Urban Studies*, Vol. 19, pp. 43-57.

Medhurst, D. and Lewis, J. (1969) *Urban Decay: An Analysis and Policy*, Macmillan, London.

Megarry, Sir R. and Wade, H. (1984) *The Law of Real Property*, Stevens, Fifth edition.

Merrett, S. (1982) *Owner Occupation in Britain*, RKP, London.

Mishra, R. (1984) *The Welfare State in Crisis: Social thought and social change*, Wheatsheaf Books, Brighton.

Monck, E. with Lomas, G. (1980) *Housing Action Areas: Success and Failure*, CES, London.

Moreton, N. and Tate, J. (1986) 'House prices in the older housing stock of Birmingham', *Housing Review*, Vol. 35, No. 3, pp. 85-87.

Morley, S. (1977) *Housing Supply*, PCL, London.

Murie, A. and Forrest, R. (1980) 'Wealth, inheritance and housing policy', *Policy and Politics*, Vol. 8, No. 1, pp. 1-19.

Nationwide Building Society (1985) *House Prices Over the Past Thirty Years*, Background Bulletin, April.

Nutt, B., Walker, B., Holliday, S. and Sear, D. (1976) *Obsolescence in Housing*, Saxon House, Farnborough.

O'Dell, A. (1979) 'An assessment of errors in a housing survey', *Urban Studies*, Vol. 17, No. 2, pp. 217-222.

Orbach, L. (1977) *Homes for Heros*, Seeley Services, London.

O'Sullivan, A. (1984) 'Misconceptions in the current housing subsidy debate', *Policy and Politics*, Vol. 12, No. 2, pp. 119-144.

Pahl, J. (1980) 'Patterns of money management within marriage', *Journal of Social Policy*, Vol. 9, No. 3, pp. 313-335.

Pahl, J. (1983) 'The allocation of money and the structuring of inequality within marriage', *Sociological Review*, Vol. 31, pp. 237-262.

Pahl, J. (1984) 'The allocation of money within the household', *The State, the Law, and the Family: Critical Perspectives*, (Freeman, M., ed.), Tavistock/Sweet and Maxwell, London, pp. 36-50.

Pahl, J. (1985) 'Who benefits from child benefit', *New Society*, Vol. 72, No. 1165, 25 April, pp. 117-119.

Paish, F. (1962) *Studies in an Inflationary Economy*, Macmillan, London.

Paris, C. and Blackaby, B. (1979) *Not Much Improvement: Urban Renewal Policy in Birmingham*, Heinemann, London.

Rae, D. (1981) *Equalities*, Harvard University Press, Cambridge, Mass.

Richardson, K. (1972) *Twentieth-Century Coventry*, Macmillan, London.

Robinson, R. (1981) 'Housing tax-expenditures subsidies and the distribution of income', *Manchester School*, XLIX, pp. 91-100.

Rothenberg, J. (1967) *Economic Evaluation of Urban Renewal*, Brookings Institute, Washington D.C.

Saunders, P. (1977) *Housing Tenure and Class Interests*, Working Paper 6, Urban and Regional Studies, University of Sussex, Brighton.

Saunders, P. (1984) 'Beyond housing classes: the sociological significance of private property rights in means of consumption', *International Journal of Urban and Regional Research*, Vol. 8, No. 2, pp. 202-227.

Saunders, P. (1986) Book review in *Housing Studies*, Vol. 1, pp. 68-70.

Shelter (1974) *Slum Clearance*, Shelter, London.

Short, J. (1982) *Housing in Britain: The Post War Experience*, Methuen, London.

Southwell, M. (1985) *Repossessions by the Halifax Building Society*, February 1984 to January 1985, Interim Report, Department of Social Policy and Health Services, University of Leeds, Leeds.

Smith, B. (1983) *Population Change in the West Midlands*, SSRC Inner City in Context Research Programme West Midlands Study Working Paper 2, Joint Centre for Regional, Urban and Local Government Studies, University of Birmingham, May.

Smith, B. (1984) *The Labour Factor as an Explanation for Economic Decline in the West Midlands Region and County: Earnings in the West Midlands*, SSRC Inner City in Context Research Programme West Midlands Study Working Paper 9, Joint Centre for Regional, Urban and Local Government Studies, University of Birmingham, May.

Stone, P. (1970) *Urban Development in Britain: Standards, Costs and Resources, 1964-2004*, Cambridge University Press, Cambridge.

Struyk, R. (1976) *Urban Home Ownership: The Economic Determinants*, Heath, Lexington, Mass.

Thorns, D. (1981) 'The implication of differential rates of capital gain from owner occupation for the formation and development of housing classes', *International Journal of Urban and Regional Research*, Vol. 5, pp. 205-217.

Thorns, D. (1982) 'Industrial restructuring and change in the labour and property markets in Britain', *Environment and Planning A*, Vol. 14, pp. 745-763.

Townsend, P. (1979) *Poverty in the United Kingdom*, Penguin, Harmondsworth.

Tunnard, J. (1976) *No Father No Home? A Study of 30 Fatherless Families in Mortgaged Homes*, Poverty Pamphlet No. 28, Child Poverty Action Group, London.

Watkins, R. and Shutt, J. (1980) *From Failure to Facelift*, CDP, Saltley, Birmingham.

Wenzlick, R. (1984) *The Real Estate Trends*, Vol. 33, No. 22, 30 June, pp. 225-232.

Whitehead, C. (1979) 'Why owner occupation?', *CES Review*, May, pp. 33-42.

Wilkinson, M. and Wilkinson, R.K. (1982) 'The withdrawal of mortgage tax relief: a survey and evaluation of the debate', *Policy and Politics*, Vol. 10, No. 1, pp. 47-64.

Wilmott, P. and Young, M. (1962) *Family and Kinship in East London*, Penguin, Harmondsworth, Middlesex.

Yates, D. (1982) 'The English housing experience: an overview', *Urban Law and Policy*, Vol. 5, No. 3, September, pp. 203-233.